J. Bildner &sons

COOKBOOK

COOKBOOK

Casual Feasts, Food on the Run, and Special Celebrations

JIM BILDNER

with *James Dodson*

Illustrated by John Burgoyne

THE HARVARD COMMON PRESS

Boston, Massachusetts

The Harvard Common Press
535 Albany Street
Boston, Massachusetts 02118

Printed in the United States of America

LIBRARY OF CONGRESS CATALOGING-IN-PUBLICATION DATA

Bildner, Jim.
    J. Bildner & Sons cookbook : casual feasts, food on the
run, and special celebrations / Jim Bildner, with James
Dodson ; illustrated by John Burgoyne
        p.   cm.
    Includes index.
    ISBN 1-55832-064-4
    1. Cookery, American.   I. J. Bildner & Sons.   II. Title.
III. Title: J. Bildner and Sons cookbook.
TX715.B4976   1993
641.5973—dc20   93-30686
                                                       CIP

Designed by Joel Avirom
Illustrations © 1988 by John Burgoyne

CONTENTS

J. Bildner & Sons

Green Awnings and a New Old-fashioned Idea

The first J. Bildner & Sons specialty grocery store opened its doors on Massachusetts Avenue in the Back Bay section of Boston just a few days before Christmas in 1984, in a restored Victorian mansion that had once belonged to the governor of the Commonwealth. The excitement was palpable as the doors swung open to a new era of Bildner's grocery stores.

A lot of tradition prepared me for that moment. My family has been associated with the merchandising of high-quality groceries for the better part of a century, and the opening of the very first J. Bildner & Sons was the happy realization of a longtime dream that my wife Nancy and I shared. We wanted to create a new kind of urban grocery store, an intimate shopping enterprise that would combine convenience and a pleasing environment with premium groceries and produce, cheeses and baked goods, fresh meats and seafoods, and an unusually broad selection of prepared take-out foods. Underscoring it all, as we envisioned it, would be some rather old-fashioned notions about customer service.

In a sense, Nancy and I were aiming to bring back something we thought was fast disappearing from the American street. We wanted to take something old and make it new. With Bildner's, we were determined to reinvent the beloved neighborhood grocery store.

In those early days, our vision went decidedly against the fashion of the times in the highly competitive grocery industry. And the same seems true today. Increasingly, mammoth superstores and "concept-killer" megastores such as Walmart, Sam's, BJ's, and other "club" stores have rendered many neighborhood food, drug, and hardware stores obsolete. The complexions of whole neighborhoods have changed as the traditional "mom and pop" stores move over to make room for the low, concrete sprawls that comprise the majority of today's food stores.

However, even though conventional retailers seem to think that consumers prefer buying five-gallon tubs of ice cream and six-pound boxes of cornflakes, recent research shows that most consumers can't possibly consume these quantities and end up throwing away large amounts of products, which, if factored into the original price, make these so-called bargains actually quite expensive.

At Bildner's, we feel that a retail food store should be visually enticing and staffed by helpful and friendly people, with a great variety of products from which customers may choose their supplies of groceries for one light snack or for a whole week's worth of hearty meals. With those goals in mind, we design our stores with classic black, green, and white tiled floors, oak trim and paneling, and glass cases that highlight the food they display and invite close inspection of the merchandise. The design and construction of the stores take a great deal of thought and work, but we hope that our efforts to create a comfortable and relaxing shopping atmosphere will make the task of grocery shopping a little more pleasant for our customers.

Our main priority, though, has been to try to develop relationships with our customers along the lines of that time-honored bond between the neighborhood grocer and his customer. We aim to provide useful information, efficient sales help, and friendly smiles to all those who walk through our doors.

Many of our beliefs were shaped by my grandfather, Joe Bildner, and my dad, Allen Bildner, and clues to my future in the grocery business were as near as my own family photo album, and as clear as the reminiscences of my grandmother, Beatrice Bildner.

My grandfather, "Mr. Joe," as he was widely known in grocery circles, opened his first grocery store in Queens, New York, in 1917. He made his mark with shoppers not only by offering the best meats and produce available, but by pioneering ideas about pricing and customer service that would become standard throughout the grocery industry.

My grandmother speaks fondly of those days—of produce clerks who were eager to assist shoppers in selecting only the best buys of the day and of friendly butchers who knew their clientele on a first-name basis and committed to memory the cuts of meat they favored.

That's the way Mr. Joe ran his operation for almost half a century. During the 1930s, Joe Bildner opened several grocery stores in northern New Jersey under the name of King's Super Market, a name that stemmed from his desire to make sure his shoppers felt like royalty. Sure, it was a bit cornball. But it was absolutely heartfelt.

Mr. Joe was a constant dreamer and grocery store innovator. His was one of the first markets anywhere to use in-store refrigerator units to keep fruits and vegetables at their peak of freshness. At a YMCA in Summit, New Jersey, he established a cooking school to help educate shoppers about food selection and preparation. An energetic and optimistic charmer, he became famous for hauling surprised customers and store employees home to dinner. To Mr. Joe, the idea of good food—both selling it and eating it—was nothing less than a daily celebration of life.

It was in this bustling environment that my father, Allen Bildner, grew up, having to keep up with the high standards and expanding ambitions of Mr. Joe. He also inherited my grandfather's generous spirit of service and built on it to guide the family enterprise into something even larger.

With my father at the helm, King's Super Markets did many things then unheard of in the grocery business. They adopted rigid standards of store cleanliness, employee relations, and product inspection that were ground-breaking in the industry. The firm was one of the first companies to place a consumer advocate on its headquarters staff, a process of direct communication between management and customers that eventually led to the establishment of special consumer panels. It wasn't quite like dragging customers home to sample Bea's lamb stew, but clearly the spirit of Mr. Joe had entered the 1970s.

I was shagging carts for my dad in those days, starting the same way every other Bildner in the grocery business had started. I worked in various departments throughout his stores. I got to know my fellow employees on a first-name basis, and I learned how things got done. The small details, I noticed, were often what counted most—meats that were a better grade or cut than the competition's, clerks that were more helpful, hours that were more convenient, and shopping aisles that were cleaner and better stocked.

By the time I was ready to embark on my own career in the

grocery business, changes in the urban American lifestyle had begun to alter significantly the way people thought about—and shopped for—food and groceries.

Studies showed that among certain kinds of shoppers—especially single working people and households where both spouses were involved with careers—demands for convenience and quality were now on a par with, and in many cases more important than, price. By the early 1980s, it was clear that a new consumer group was emerging whose needs and tastes were limited only by their busy work schedules.

The highly specialized food services were welcomed, to be sure. For a while, it seemed like there was a new pasta shop or French bakery opening on every other street corner in urban America. The problem was, modern life demanded more than lots of places to buy fresh tortellini or toasty croissants. As we viewed it, there was no reason why a small grocery store couldn't offer the very best of everything from arugula to Ajax, from fresh pasta to paper towels. We felt there was room in the market for a return of the neighborhood store. We hoped the public would agree.

The response was, to say the least, immensely gratifying.

The food press in Boston greeted us warmly. But there was some intriguing confusion. Certain newspaper and magazine critics didn't quite know how to peg us. To some, J. Bildner & Sons was a specialty grocery store that offered, as a bonus, gourmet take-out cuisine—food as good as that served in most distinctive restaurants. To others, Bildner's was a gourmet food emporium that also sold bathtub cleanser and cat food. One memorable review called us a New Age convenience store. Another critic was impressed by our range of household items, gourmet cheeses, and baked goods, but focused on our distinctive green awnings and beautiful premises and the surprisingly old-fashioned way in which we went about our tasks. He called it "grocery shopping as theater . . . a new consumer art form."

They were all quite correct. Despite attempts to categorize our appeal, J. Bildner & Sons was many things to many people—a great deli, a reliable grocery store, the perfect place to pick up fresh flowers, buy a French *boule* and a chunk of flawless aged Camembert, rent a classic video, or order an elegant dinner for six. Our goal was to offer only the best of a variety of things. That we catered anything from a picnic for two in the Public Garden to a formal dinner for fifty only added to the store's unusual appeal.

Today, we still think that formula works. And although it's no secret that, like many other enterprises, we got caught in the web of the fast-growth '80s, I think we have used the lesson to re-emphasize and strengthen the intimate feel that we set out to create when we opened the first store. So five years, two children, two dogs, and a smaller 1990s house later, I find myself writing this new introduction to our cookbook's second edition.

The impetus behind this new edition of the *J. Bildner & Sons Cookbook* is the same as it was when we first published it in 1988. What we hear from our customers today indicates that consumer knowledge of food is better than ever and interest in food preparation at home is stronger than it has been in years. People are concerned about the nutritional value of what they are eating, and they want a delicious home-cooked meal that they can share with their families and friends in the comfort of their own kitchens.

So we set out to write a cookbook that addressed a wide range of moments in the modern lifestyle when the presentation of good food—just the right dish—can make all the difference. We wanted a cookbook that offered simple yet sophisticated recipes that would provide easy solutions to the many dining challenges that arise. For that reason, the book is thematically arranged according to specific occasions, rather than traditional courses. For instance, in place of chapters devoted to meats, poultry, and fish entrees, you will find recipes grouped under, say, "For Friends and Lovers" or "Video Victuals" or "Taking the Show Outside."

Since its first publication in 1988, some eight million customers have come through our store doors, sampling, eating, browsing, commenting, and helping us understand changing American tastes. Trends have come, gone, and come again. Thai, Tex-Mex, Southwest, Comfort Foods, Sushi, Nouvelle, Lite, Mediterranean, and California cuisines have all influenced our recipes over the past five years. Among all these changes, one thing remains abundantly clear—we are all culinary explorers. Our tastes are ever-changing, constantly seeking new flavors, new culinary cultures, new ways to experience other parts of our rapidly shrinking world. Still, in all, nothing has changed the simple pleasure of a good meal, prepared well, served at home in intimate surroundings with friends and family.

Our stores and our philosophy remain committed to this fact. As the retail food service industry continues to fragment with mass marketers and so-called warehouse stores on one end, we happily take our position on the other end, providing foods and services to customers who enjoy food. As we search out recipes for this book and the next, Nancy and I are mindful that the world of the 1990s is quite different from that of the 1980s. Not only is time more scarce, but quality time is more precious than ever. As you read through this book, I hope it will affirm for you what it does for us. Some of the best moments in life occur at family dinners, picnics with friends, or those all too rare romantic dinners alone. We hope our book will serve as a kitchen companion for those special moments. In the meantime, rest assured that we will be looking for the next set of special recipes. Enjoy!

Many talented people contributed their expertise to the effort behind the first edition of this cookbook, and I'd like to acknowledge their hard work: Alison MacDonald Dodson, Deirdre Davis, Jim Dodson, Steven Petusevsky, Linda Upright, Mike Billings, Celia Rodrigues, Jane Maxwell, Paul Abramsky, Ann Stark, Susan Peery, Emmy Purdy, Terry Bartow, and Lisa Kelly. And for the publication of this new edition, I am happy to thank my literary agent, Doe Coover, and Bruce Shaw of the Harvard Common Press.

I have three final people to thank. First, my dad. His inspiration helped instill an appreciation for the quality of food and respect for the customer. To my wife, Nancy, whose patience and care make it possible for me to devote the necessary time to running the business. Finally, Mr. Joe, the original family dreamer. Strange as it may sound, I tend to think—no, let me say I sincerely hope—that his generous spirit of loving good food is still with us. I have an image of him, somewhere in the stars, getting ready to open a small neighborhood grocery store . . .

Like him, when it comes to good food, I spend a lot of time dreaming.

NOTES ON INGREDIENTS

Flour means unsifted general-purpose flour unless other-wise indicated.

If heavy cream is not available in your part of the country, substitute whipping cream.

Sugar means granulated white sugar.

Freshly ground pepper means black pepper unless other-wise indicated.

We generally prefer fresh ingredients (like fresh lemon juice and fresh vegetables) to canned or bottled.

The Casual Feast

Our gourmet take-out counters do their busiest trade during stretches of beautiful summer weather, or when there is an outdoor symphony concert scheduled, or on weekends when a big football game is going on somewhere in town. We've noticed the same thing tends to happen whenever one of those government holidays rolls around and everyone (everyone, that is, except us) takes a Monday off to sleep in, lounge around the house, or make a run for the nearest beach. We've even found that a great movie premiering on cable TV stimulates take-out sales.

These observations tell us there are a lot of small moments in your busy life when you want a casual feast to place on your table (or picnic blanket) for friends and family—yet don't want to make a big fuss out of the whole affair.

In this decidedly informal first section, we'll focus on casual occasions of many kinds—like an alfresco dinner at the summer bandshell, a tailgate bash before the big game, or a stay-at-home Saturday night for two in front of the VCR.

A customer of ours who loves to entertain contends that a special breakfast or brunch for overnight guests is the most challenging meal to bring off. It seems like you never even give breakfast a thought until suddenly it's time to throw something great together. You can't always just turn on the creativity with the gas range.

We know what she means, and then some. You might have entertained the night before and friends from the country made a snap decision to sleep over. You're the first soul up—first to put on the coffee and collect the Sunday morning paper, and first to try and whip up some culinary inspiration for breakfast. Or there are the times you're called on to put together a super brunch for friends, or lay out a holiday breakfast for the family. Then, too, there is that special rainy evening you're the first one

home from work and decide to pull a switcheroo and serve breakfast for dinner.

The unique recipes found in this chapter will answer an ardent breakfast lover's needs. The dishes we've developed are perfect for entertaining guests—and equally suitable for solitary mornings, when a little breakfast self-indulgence is in order. In most cases, these are relatively simple dishes that require a minimum of time and labor and use inexpensive ingredients likely to be found in any good kitchen, at any time.

More important, they will go a long way toward helping to make even the simplest breakfast offering a great beginning.

Corn, Brie, and Jalapeño Frittata

YIELD: 4 SERVINGS

*T*his spunky brunch dish, a kind of open-faced omelet, also makes a wonderful late night dinner. Extra diced Brie can be saved and kept frozen in a container—it's great to have on hand to add to sauces and omelets.

1 (6-ounce) wedge Brie
1 medium onion
2 medium jalapeño peppers, fresh or canned
6 whole fresh basil leaves
3 tablespoons butter
¾ cup corn kernels, fresh or frozen and thawed
5 eggs
Salt and freshly ground pepper to taste

1. Place the Brie in the freezer to make it easier to dice.

2. Finely dice the onion. Steam (if fresh), core, and seed the jalapeño peppers and mince them finely (⅛-inch pieces). (Wear rubber gloves when working with jalapeño peppers to prevent irritation.)

3. Stack the basil leaves on top of one another and roll them from the long side into a cigar shape. Cut the rolled leaves into shreds as thin as possible.

4. In a small heavy skillet, melt 1 tablespoon of the butter over medium heat. Add the onion and sauté, stirring, for 3 minutes. Add the jalapeños and the corn kernels and reduce heat to low. Sauté until the corn is tender, about 5 minutes. Cool slightly.

5. While the mixture is cooling, cut the chilled Brie lengthwise into ¼-inch slices. Cut the slices in half again lengthwise. Cut those strips crosswise into ¼-inch pieces. You'll end up with ¼ × ⅛-inch rectangles. (If the cheese starts to get warm and hard to work with, place it back in the freezer for a few minutes.)

6. In a medium bowl, beat the eggs lightly with a whisk. Add the cooled corn mixture, diced Brie, salt, and pepper. Stir to combine.

7. Preheat the broiler.

8. In an ovenproof skillet, melt the remaining 2 tablespoons of butter over medium-high heat. Add the egg mixture to the skillet. Using a metal spatula, lift the edges of the egg mixture as they cook, and tip the skillet slightly to allow uncooked egg to flow underneath. Continue to do this until all the edges are set, about 1 minute. Do not stir.

9. Reduce the heat to low, cover the skillet, and cook until the eggs are almost set, about 5 minutes.

10. Uncover the skillet and place it under the broiler. Broil the frittata until the top is golden brown, watching carefully to see that it doesn't burn. Garnish with the shredded basil and serve.

MIX INTO YOUR SCRAMBLED EGGS . . .

- slices of smoked sausage and chunks of diced red and green peppers
- jalapeños, tomatoes, and corn kernels
- Hot salsa and Monterey Jack cheese
- Smoked salmon and sorrel
- Asparagus tips and fresh crabmeat with a sprinkle of Cheddar
- Diced ham and Brie
- Feta cheese, chopped Bermuda onion, dried tomatoes

A Romantic Russian Omelet

YIELD: 2 SERVINGS

Here's an example of gourmet *glasnost*, a fluffy omelet filled with tiny scallops, black caviar, and a hint of lemon. Great for a romantic brunch or a late night wintry Russian supper—especially when served with very chilled vodka. The technique we outline here to make the omelet appears much more complicated than it really is.

½ pound bay scallops
3 tablespoons butter
Salt and freshly ground pepper to taste
4 eggs
2 tablespoons heavy cream
2 teaspoons black caviar
2 tablespoons sour cream
¼ teaspoon grated lemon rind

1. Remove the tough tendon from the outer side of the scallops. Cut the scallops in half through the center, making 2 thin discs.

2. Melt 1 tablespoon of the butter in a small skillet over high heat. Sauté the scallops quickly, stirring, for 1 to 2 minutes, until opaque. Remove from the heat and season with salt and pepper.

3. Beat together 2 of the eggs, 1 tablespoon of the heavy cream, and salt and pepper to taste. Melt 1 tablespoon of the remaining butter in an omelet pan over high heat. Pour the egg mixture into the hot pan, count to eight, then beat it lightly with a fork while it cooks.

4. When the egg is almost set, slide it to the far side of the pan so that it curves up the edge opposite you. Using a spatula, smooth the egg to make a flat surface with no holes. Remove the pan from the heat.

5. Place half the sautéed scallops in the center of the omelet. Top them with 1 teaspoon of the caviar. Fold the third of the omelet that is closest to you over the filling and fold the third of the omelet that is farthest from you over the first folded side. Invert the omelet onto a plate, seam-side down. Spread the top with 1 tablespoon of the sour cream and sprinkle with half of the lemon rind. (This whole process should take between 30 and 60 seconds.)

6. Repeat with remaining ingredients, making a second complete omelet.

Italian Bacon and Eggs

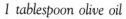

YIELD: 2 SERVINGS

Most alternatives to the traditional American morning combo are fairly complicated affairs. This one, however, is almost as easy to prepare as it is robust and satisfying. Served with a side dish of Hot Potato Pepper Salad (recipe follows), it is a great change-of-pace Sunday brunch.

1 tablespoon olive oil
4 slices pancetta (Italian bacon, available at Italian markets and most delis)
4 eggs
1 tablespoon chopped fresh Italian parsley

1. Heat the olive oil in a large skillet over high heat. Add the pancetta in a single layer and cook 5 minutes, turning once.

2. Carefully break 1 egg on each pancetta slice. Sprinkle each with chopped parsley.

3. Cover the pan, reduce the heat to medium, and cook until the egg yolk is cooked as desired (3 minutes for medium, 5 minutes for well cooked). Serve immediately.

Hot Potato Pepper Salad

YIELD: 4 SERVINGS

*T*his spicy recipe was developed for us by Wild Thyme Farm, which makes lovely flavored vinegars and cooking oils. It's a superb companion to Italian Bacon and Eggs (see preceding recipe), but may also be served as a luncheon dish or as a companion to a steak dinner.

1 pound small red new potatoes (the size of golf balls),
    unpeeled
1 medium stalk celery
1 medium leek (white part only)
4 scallions (green tops only)
¼ cup diced red bell pepper
¼ cup diced green bell pepper
¼ cup diced red onion
4 slices bacon
6 tablespoons Wild Thyme Farm Hot Pepper Vinegar (see
    note)
1 teaspoon paprika
Salt and freshly ground pepper to taste

NOTE: Wild Thyme Farm's Hot Pepper Vinegar can be found in many specialty food markets. But if it is not available, you may substitute a mixture of ⅛ teaspoon cayenne pepper and 3 to 4 drops of Tabasco sauce added to 6 tablespoons red wine or cider vinegar.

1. Steam or boil the potatoes until tender (10 to 15 minutes). Rinse them in cold water and set aside to cool.

2. Dice the celery and leek. Cut the scallion tops into ¼-inch slices. Place all three in a bowl with the diced red pepper, green pepper, and red onion.

3. In a medium skillet, over high heat, sauté the bacon slices until crisp. Drain on a paper towel.

4. Pour the excess fat from the pan and return it to the heat. When hot, deglaze it with the hot pepper vinegar. Add the paprika and let the mixture bubble for 2 to 3 minutes. Remove the pan from the heat.

5. Quarter the cooled potatoes and add them to the bowl of chopped vegetables. Salt and pepper to taste.

6. Pour the hot vinaigrette over the potato-vegetable mixture and toss. Crumble the bacon over the top and serve immediately.

FRENCH TOAST VARIATIONS

LEFTOVER BREAD	ADD TO EGG MIXTURE	TOP WITH
Oatmeal bread	2 teaspoons brown sugar 1 teaspoon cinnamon	Sliced apples sautéed in butter and apple brandy
Croissants	1 teaspoon lemon rind	Fresh strawberries and lightly whipped cream
Anadama (cornmeal-and-molasses bread)	1 tablespoon molasses	fresh blueberries boiled briefly with a little water and sugar
Sourdough	¼ teaspoon white pepper ½ teaspoon black pepper	mushrooms sautéed in butter and deglazed with a little cream
Baguettes, sliced crosswise into "silver dollars"	1 tablespoon bourbon	bananas and pecans sautéed in butter and brown sugar
Cranberry bread	2 tablespoons orange juice	orange syrup made by boiling and reducing orange juice, lemon juice, and sugar

Sunday French Toast

YIELD: 6 SERVINGS

*A*nyone who has more than a passing fancy for the delicate flavor of famous New Orleans beignets will find this spruced-up variation of an old standard quite pleasing. Sunday French Toast can be served equally well with maple syrup, honey, sugar and cinnamon, or any of your other favorite toppings for french toast or pancakes. Serve with a side dish of yogurt garnished with fresh fruit to give a nice balance to the sweet fried dough.

6 thick (at least 1-inch) slices white bakery-style or
   homemade bread
2 cups flour
4 teaspoons baking powder
½ cup sugar
Salt to taste
1 large egg, beaten slightly
1½ cups milk
1 tablespoon butter, melted
1 teaspoon vanilla
Vegetable oil for frying
Maple syrup, honey, or sugar and cinnamon for topping

1. Preheat the oven to 200°F. Quarter the bread slices diagonally and trim the crusts. Leave the bread to dry overnight, or spread the slices on a baking sheet and place them in the preheated oven to dry for 5 to 10 minutes. Do not turn the oven off.

2. Combine the flour, baking powder, sugar, and salt in a large bowl. Whisk in the beaten egg, milk, melted butter, and vanilla.

3. Heat 2 to 3 inches of vegetable oil in a large saucepan or deep fryer until hot but not smoking (about 375°F.)

4. Dip the bread slices in the batter, coating them completely. Fry them in the hot oil in small batches (4 to 6 at a time, depending on the size of the saucepan or fryer) for about 30 seconds on each side, until golden.

5. Drain the bread on paper towels and keep the first batches hot by placing them in the oven while you fry the remainder. When you have finished frying all the toast, serve immediately. Pass maple syrup, honey, or sugar and cinnamon to top the toast.

Peachy-Cheese Jamboree Pancakes

YIELD: 2 TO 4 SERVINGS

*T*his peppy breakfast variation is not too sweet, and has a buoyant gingery flavor. We love it served with blueberries or stewed apples, to complete the fruit jamboree.

2 medium fresh peaches (see note)
½ cup water
1½ × 3-inch strip lemon rind
¾ cup sugar
2 cups cottage cheese
1 tablespoon lemon juice
¼ teaspoon salt
½ teaspoon grated lemon rind
1 teaspoon powdered ginger
1 cup flour
3 tablespoons butter
Sour cream for topping

NOTE: *You may substitute canned, juice-packed peaches for fresh. Just omit the water and reduce the sugar in the poaching syrup to ¼ cup (use ½ cup sugar for the recipe in total).*

1. Preheat the oven to 200° F.

2. Peel the peaches with a sharp paring knife and slice them into 8 slices each. Place the water, strip of lemon rind, and ½ cup of the sugar in a medium saucepan. Bring the liquid to a boil. Add the peach slices, lower the heat, and simmer for 5 minutes. Remove the pan from the heat and set aside.

3. Place the cottage cheese in the bowl of a food processor fitted with a steel blade. Process the cheese until it is smooth and creamy. (This can also be done with an electric mixer or blender, but the batter will not be as smooth.) Add the lemon juice, remaining ¼ cup sugar, salt, grated lemon rind, and ginger. Process until smooth. Add the flour and process just enough to blend.

4. Melt 1 tablespoon of the butter in a large skillet over medium heat. Drop the batter in large spoonfuls (about ¼ cup)—4 at a time—into the skillet. Fry them, turning once, until golden.

5. Continue frying 4 pancakes at a time, using 1 table-spoon of butter for each batch. (The batter makes twelve 3- to 4-inch pancakes, so three batches should do it.) Keep the cooked pancakes warm in a low oven.

6. To serve, pour some of the warm peach sauce over each serving of pancakes. Top each serving with a dollop of sour cream.

Down-Home Waffles

You need only one sweet potato and one apple to make this breakfast crowd pleaser. Since the other ingredients are likely to be as close as your pantry shelf, you don't really have to plan ahead to make it. Lyle's Golden Syrup is worth substituting for regular maple syrup, because maple syrup tends to overpower the sweet potato and apple flavors. It can be found in the imported food section of most supermarkets.

1 small sweet potato
1 small tart apple, such as McIntosh
¼ cup butter
½ teaspoon ground cinnamon
¼ teaspoon ground nutmeg
1½ cups flour
¼ cup sugar
1 tablespoon baking powder
½ teaspoon salt
4 eggs
2 cups milk
Lyle's Golden Syrup or maple syrup
2 tablespoons butter (optional)

1. Peel the sweet potato and apple and cut both into 1- to 2-inch chunks. Place them in a medium saucepan, cover with water and cook over medium-high heat until they are soft when pierced with a knife (about 10 minutes). Drain well, then add the ¼ cup butter, cinnamon, and nutmeg and mash together, using a potato masher.

2. Sift the flour, sugar, baking powder, and salt together into a large bowl.

HOW TO BUY COFFEE

Sometimes it can be a little daunting to stand at a gourmet coffee counter—you'd like to try something a bit different, but the strange names are intimidating and most of the blends sound too dessertlike for your morning pot. Here are some hints:

ROASTS

In general, the longer the roast, the darker the bean and the deeper—though not necessarily the stronger—the flavor.
- Regular or American: a medium-brown bean
- Viennese: darker, with a slightly oily surface
- French: even darker, with an oily surface
- Italian espresso or dark French roast: almost black, with a shiny, oily surface

COUNTRIES OF ORIGIN
- Rich: Kenyan AA, Colombian Supremo, Sumatra Mandheling, Kona
- Mellow: Antigua Guatemalan, Ethiopian Harrar, Mexican Altura
- Light: Andean Peru, Brazil Santos

3. In a separate medium bowl, beat the eggs until fluffy. While continuing to beat, gradually add the milk. Beat well.

4. Using a spoon, make a well in the center of the flour mixture. Add half the beaten egg mixture and all of the sweet potato mixture and mix well. Add the second half of the beaten egg mixture and mix.

5. Heat the syrup in a small saucepan over low heat. Add 2 tablespoons butter, if desired.

6. Bake the waffles according to the waffle iron directions. Serve with the warm syrup.

Southwestern
Souffléed Tomatoes

YIELD: 6 SERVINGS

A relaxed weekend morning is an ideal time to try some creative cooking. As with any soufflé, the key here is to serve the dish while it's still puffy and warm. If you prepare it slightly differently, it makes a delicious hors d'oeuvre (see note).

6 medium firm tomatoes (about 3 inches in diameter)
12 ounces Monterey Jack cheese, flavored with jalapeños or
  hot peppers if available
¼ cup cornmeal
1 clove garlic
½ teaspoon ground cumin
½ teaspoon dried oregano
1 tablespoon chopped fresh coriander (cilantro)
Dash of Tabasco sauce
1 egg, separated
1 egg white
Oil for baking sheet

1. Preheat the oven to 450° F.

2. Core the tomatoes and cut a thin slice off each top. Remove the pulp and seeds with a small spoon.

3. Grate the cheese and place it in a medium bowl. Mix in the cornmeal.

4. Mince the garlic and add it to the cheese mixture, along with the cumin, oregano, coriander, and Tabasco sauce. Add the egg yolk and blend.

5. Place the 2 egg whites in a separate medium bowl. Beat the whites until firm but not dry. Stir one third of the whites into the cheese mixture, then fold in the remaining two thirds with a spatula or flat spoon.

6. Spoon about ½ cup of the mixture into the center of each tomato.

7. Lightly oil a cookie sheet or jelly roll pan. Place the tomatoes on the oiled sheet and bake them for about 15 minutes, or until puffed and golden. (Very ripe tomatoes may split somewhat as they bake.) Serve immediately.

NOTE: *To make Southwestern Cherry Tomatoes for an hors d'oeuvre, cut the quantities for the filling in half (but still use 1 whole egg yolk). Fill 40 to 50 (about 2 pint boxes) hollowed-out cherry tomatoes with 1 to 1½ teaspoons of filling each. Bake them in a preheated 450° F oven for 8 to 10 minutes.*

Baked Grits with Chives

YIELD: 6 SERVINGS

*I*f you've ever eaten breakfast in a highway truck stop in Dixie, you know how commonplace—and beloved—is the humble bowl of grits. Before you shake your head, give this dressed-up version of the Southern Everyman classic a chance to delight and surprise your guests at your next brunch or weekend breakfast. It's easy and fast and goes with anything from steak and fried eggs to crab-stuffed omelets.

4½ tablespoons butter
3 cups water
1 cup milk
1 cup quick-cooking grits
1 teaspoon salt
3 ounces cream cheese
½ cup sour cream
3 eggs
¼ cup snipped fresh chives
Freshly ground pepper to taste

1. Preheat the oven to 325° F.

2. Using ½ tablespoon of the butter, butter the bottom and sides of a 2-quart baking dish.

3. Pour the water and ¾ cup of the milk into a medium-size heavy saucepan and bring it to a boil over high heat. As soon as it starts to boil, slowly begin to add the grits, whisking constantly. Continue to whisk and bring the mixture back to the boil.

4. When the mixture just begins to boil again, add the salt and lower the heat to medium. Cook, stirring with a wooden spoon, for 5 to 10 minutes.

5. When the grits are thick, remove the pan from the heat and add the remaining 4 tablespoons of butter and the cream cheese. Stir until both the butter and the cheese are melted.

6. Place the sour cream in a small bowl. Add the eggs and beat to combine. Add the remaining ¼ cup milk. Slowly pour the sour cream mixture into the hot grits, stirring constantly. Stir in the snipped chives and black pepper.

7. Pour the grits mixture into the prepared dish. Place it in the oven to bake for 45 minutes to 1 hour, until the top is golden. Serve immediately.

Quick Bacon Bread

YIELD: 1 (8-INCH) LOAF

*T*he night before a brunch is the perfect time to bake this unusual quick bread, which can become part of everything from Bildner Benedict (see Index) to a classic BLT. Or simply toast it lightly and serve it with scrambled eggs and fruit on the side.

1 teaspoon butter or vegetable oil for loaf pan
1 pound high-quality bacon (not too fatty)
2 cups flour
2 tablespoons sugar
2 teaspoons baking powder
1 teaspoon baking soda
¾ teaspoon salt
¼ teaspoon freshly ground black pepper
2 eggs
¼ cup milk
1 cup sour cream

1. Preheat the oven to 350° F.

2. Grease an 8¼ × 4½-inch loaf pan with 1 teaspoon butter or vegetable oil.

3. Cook the bacon—in batches if necessary—in a large skillet over high heat until crisp. Place it on paper towels to drain and cool. Reserve 2 tablespoons of the bacon fat from the skillet. Crumble the bacon.

4. In a large mixing bowl, combine the flour, sugar, baking powder, baking soda, salt, and pepper.

5. In a small bowl, beat the eggs slightly. Whisk in the milk and sour cream. Add the reserved bacon fat and mix until smooth. Pour the egg mixture into the dry ingredients. Add the reserved crumbled bacon and stir just to combine (the batter can be slightly lumpy).

6. Pour the batter into the prepared loaf pan and bake for 50 minutes to 1 hour, until a skewer inserted in the center of the loaf comes out clean and dry. Let the bread cool in the pan for 5 to 10 minutes, then turn it out onto a rack to cool. Allow the bread to cool completely, then store it wrapped tightly in foil or plastic wrap, at room temperature. Serve toasted.

Noir Comme le diable	Black as the Devil
Chaud comme l'enfer	Hot as Hell
Pur comme un ange,	Pure as an angel
Doux comme l'amour	Sweet as Love

—A popular inscription found on old coffeepots, attributed to Charles Maurice de Talleyrand-Périgord

Golden Island Scones

YIELD: 12 SCONES

*A*mong the many tastes we've picked up from the oh-so-proper British of late is an affection for the humble breakfast tidbits, scones. Ours are properly not too sweet and are very triangular, in other words very correct for high tea, or simply for a light breakfast with scrambled eggs. They call to mind the golden time when Britannia still ruled the waves.

2 cups flour
2 teaspoons baking powder
¼ cup sugar
¼ teaspoon salt
4 tablespoons plus ½ tablespoon butter
2 eggs
1 cup crushed, drained pineapple (reserve ¼ cup juice)
⅓ cup light cream
3 tablespoons brown sugar

1. Preheat the oven to 425° F.

2. Sift the flour, baking powder, sugar, and salt into a large bowl. Using a pastry blender or 2 knives, cut 4 tablespoons of the butter into the flour mixture.

3. Add the eggs, crushed pineapple, and cream. Using a wooden spoon, mix thoroughly but quickly (do not overbeat), pressing the dough together with your hands if necessary. The dough should be slightly soft, but it should hold together and not be sticky.

4. Turn the dough out onto a floured board. Roll it or gently pat it into a ½- to ¾-inch-thick rectangle.

5. Cut the rectangle crosswise into thirds. Cut an X in each third, to make 12 triangles. Place the triangles on a baking sheet buttered with the remaining ½ tablespoon of butter.

6. Brush the reserved pineapple juice over the tops of the scones. Sprinkle them lightly with the brown sugar. Bake for 10 to 12 minutes, until golden brown.

McSteven's Cocoa Muffins

YIELD: 12 MUFFINS

*T*he muffin craze seems to be here to stay—in our stores alone we sell over two thousand a day—and this rich, sour cream concoction is a most unusual muffin. If McSteven's Spicy Cherry Cocoa is not available, the substitute mixture will give the muffins the proper zing. They are a lovely late breakfast or afternoon snack when heated slightly and served with hot, lemony tea.

12 muffin papers or oil for muffin tin
1 (3-ounce) bar white chocolate
6 tablespoons butter
1⅓ cups flour
⅓ cup McSteven's Spicy Cherry Cocoa (see note)
1 tablespoon baking powder
½ teaspoon salt
1 egg
1 cup sour cream
½ cup milk
½ cup sugar

NOTE: McSteven's line of spiced and flavored cocoas can be found in most specialty food markets. If it is not available, substitute this mixture: ⅓ cup unsweetened cocoa, 1 teaspoon ground cinnamon, ½ teaspoon ground allspice, and ½ teaspoon ground nutmeg.

1. Preheat the oven to 350° F.

2. Prepare the muffin tin by lining it with muffin papers or by brushing the muffin cups lightly with oil.

3. Cut the white chocolate into small pieces and set aside.

4. Melt the butter over low heat. Set aside to cool.

5. Sift into a medium bowl the flour, cocoa, baking powder, and salt.

6. In a separate medium bowl, whisk the egg lightly. Gradually whisk the melted butter into the egg. Add the sour cream, milk, and sugar and beat until well blended.

7. Add the liquid ingredients and the white chocolate pieces to the dry ingredients. Stir just to combine.

8. Fill each muffin cup with batter to three-quarters full. Bake for 15 to 20 minutes, or until a skewer inserted in the center of the muffins comes out clean and dry. Serve warm.

BREAKFAST IN THE WILD

Saturday morning breakfast: Early summer mornings, when the sun is bright but the air is still a little crisp (and none of the summer insects are out yet) is the perfect time for breakfast on the deck, patio, or yard. Keep it simple, though—just fill a tray with coffee or tea, juice, and a treat to linger over, like Golden Island Scones with lime marmalade, or McSteven's Cocoa Muffins, or Lemon Pear Bread with lemon curd and cream cheese. (Somehow, anything sinful seems a little more innocent in the great outdoors.)

*T*he best weekends are made of blue jeans and sneakers, great meals, and your favorite people. Weekends are that much-needed time you share with friends and family, so the food you serve should reflect that casual attitude but, like them, also be something a bit special.

In this home and hearth chapter we'll take several casual dinner classics, give them an interesting twist, and add a handful of new ideas to enliven the festive nature of any weekend dinner table.

Most of these recipes can be prepared without a lot of advance preparation and bother, saving you time to be with friends or family. They're great for that weekend of the first snowfall, the busy graduation weekend, or the weekend the folks come to see the new baby.

Marinated Tortellini with Basil-Sour Cream Dip

YIELD: 8 TO 12 SERVINGS

*H*ere's what we call good "stalling" food—just the thing to keep folks occupied as they're hanging around the kitchen talking and sipping wine before dinner. This great hors d'oeuvre is not too fancy but it is tasty and fun. You can make it the night before and chill it, which makes life even easier.

TORTELLINI:
1 pound cheese-stuffed tortellini (a mixture of spinach pasta and plain pasta is nice)
1 teaspoon salt for cooking water
4 tablespoons olive oil
2 tablespoons lemon juice

BASIL-SOUR CREAM DIP:
½ cup sliced almonds
¼ cup grated Parmesan cheese
½ cup chopped fresh basil
1½ cups sour cream
Salt to taste
Freshly ground white pepper to taste
3 tablespoons lemon juice

1. Cook the noodles in a large pot of salted water according to package directions, until tender. Drain the pasta and place it in a large bowl. Sprinkle with the olive oil and 2 tablespoons of the lemon juice and toss to coat. Set aside to marinate (refrigerate if storing overnight).

2. To make the dip, grind the sliced almonds in a blender or food processor fitted with a steel blade. Place the ground almonds in a small bowl and stir in the grated Parmesan, chopped basil, and sour cream. Add the salt, white pepper, and 3 tablespoons of lemon juice. Stir to blend, then cover and chill for several hours or overnight to give the flavors a chance to blend.

3. Serve the tortellini with toothpicks to dip in the sour cream dip.

Chicken Liver Apple Pâté with Cognac

YIELD: 2 CUPS

Here's a superb appetizer that can be made ahead of time and simply taken out of the fridge and served on a tray with crackers or French bread when weekend guests arrive. The combination of apple and cognac has a light, sweet essence that goes well with almost any dry wine.

½ cup heavy cream, chilled
1 pound chicken livers
1 tart apple, such as Granny Smith
1 small onion
2 cups chicken stock
2 cups water
½ cup butter, room temperature
Salt and freshly ground pepper to taste
½ teaspoon freshly grated nutmeg
2 tablespoons cognac

1. Pour the cream into a medium bowl and beat just until soft peaks begin to form. Refrigerate.

2. Clean the chicken livers of veins and fat. Set aside.

3. Peel, quarter, and core the apple. Slice it crosswise into ½-inch pieces. Set aside.

4. Cut the onion into ⅓-inch slices. Set aside.

5. Pour the chicken stock and water into a medium saucepan. Place the pan over high heat and bring the liquid to a boil. Add the apple and onion slices and boil for 5 minutes. Add the chicken livers, reduce the heat to moderate, and simmer, covered, for 8 minutes. Drain and set aside to cool for 15 minutes.

6. Place the drained chicken liver mixture in a food processor fitted with a steel blade. Purée until smooth. Add butter, salt, pepper, nutmeg, and cognac. Blend until smooth.

7. Transfer the mixture to a large bowl. Remove the whipped cream from the refrigerator and whisk lightly to reblend. Gently fold the whipped cream into the chicken liver purée, until no streaks of white remain. Pack the pâté into a crock or mold, cover, and chill for at least one hour, or until firm. Serve with thin slices of French bread or crackers.

Cajun Meatloaf

YIELD: 6 TO 8 SERVINGS

Steve Petusevsky, our executive chef at Bildner's, loves to take a classic recipe and creatively fiddle with the ingredients until a terrific new version of a wonderful old standard results. This recipe is a first-rate example of masterful fiddling—and is one of the most popular take-out items sold in our stores. Our chef points out that the same recipe may be used to make Cajun Meatballs, which makes a spectacular hors d'oeuvres or a spicy side dish for breakfast or brunch. (Just shape the meatloaf mixture into small balls and fry in a small amount of oil until browned.)

5 large eggs
2 medium stalks celery
2 medium onions
2 cloves garlic
1½ pounds extra lean ground beef
½ pound ground pork
1½ teaspoons ground cumin
1½ teaspoons ground coriander
2 teaspoons dried oregano (or ¼ cup chopped fresh)
1 teaspoon dried thyme (or 2 teaspoons chopped fresh)
½ teaspoon cayenne pepper
1½ teaspoons salt
½ teaspoon freshly ground pepper
½ teaspoon red pepper flakes (optional)
1 cup unseasoned bread crumbs
½ cup milk
¼ cup chutney, such as Major Grey's

1. Preheat the oven to 425° F.

2. Place 3 eggs in a small saucepan and cover them with water. Place the saucepan over high heat and bring the water to a boil. Cover the pan, remove it from the heat, and then let the eggs sit in the hot water for 20 minutes. Drain the eggs and rinse under cold water to cool. Peel them and set aside.

3. While the eggs are cooking, chop the celery and onion into ⅓-inch dice. Mince the garlic cloves finely. Place the celery, onion, and garlic in a large bowl.

4. Add the ground beef and pork to the celery mixture and mix well. Sprinkle the cumin, coriander, oregano, thyme, cayenne pepper, salt, and black pepper over the meat and mix to blend. Add the red pepper flakes, if desired. Add the remaining 2 raw eggs, the bread crumbs, and the milk and mix everything together thoroughly, using your hands.

5. Place half the meat mixture in a layer in a 9 × 5-inch loaf pan. Place the peeled, hard-cooked eggs end-to-end, along the center of the pan, on top of the meat. Push them down gently to embed them slightly in the meat mixture. Cover the eggs with the remaining meat mixture, pressing it lightly in and around the eggs to seal. Score the top of the meatloaf with a fork and spread the chutney evenly over the meat.

6. Bake until the loaf is firm and the juices are bubbling, about 45 minutes.

TRENDS WE'D LIKE TO SEE IN THE 1990s

Traditional cooking methods
Classic dinners
Homemade gravies
More Southwestern cuisine
Lunches brought from home
Creative leftovers
Homemade beer
Potluck suppers
Kefir
Lemon curd
Scottish cookery
Oversized spatulas
White tablecloths
Simple bread recipes
Fewer kitchen gadgets
Automobiles equipped with
   microwave ovens
Expensive restaurants with
   friendly waiters
Cleaner tapwater
Mandatory cooking classes for
   college students
Home canning
New uses for beets, cabbage,
   and parsnips

Irish Lasagna

YIELD: 10 SERVINGS

*T*his weekend dinner recipe is great for entertaining because it is different and good and makes enough to feed a small army. The extra sauce can be refrigerated and used with pasta later in the week.

3 pounds boiling potatoes (about 5 large)
4 large cloves garlic
3 tablespoons olive oil
2 pounds extra lean ground beef
2 teaspoons dried basil (or 4 tablespoons chopped fresh)
2 teaspoons dried oregano (or 4 tablespoons chopped fresh)
½ teaspoon red pepper flakes
1 teaspoon salt plus additional to taste for sprinkling layers
2 (32-ounce) jars chunky meatless spaghetti sauce
1½ cups water
1½ pounds mozzarella cheese
Freshly ground pepper to taste

1. Preheat the oven to 350° F.

2. Bring a large pot of water to a boil. Peel the potatoes and cut them into ¼-inch slices. Blanch the potatoes in the boiling water for 5 minutes. Remove the pot from the heat but do not drain the potatoes. Set aside.

3. Mince the garlic finely.

4. Pour 1 tablespoon of the olive oil into a large saucepan and place the pan over high heat. Add the ground beef to the hot oil and brown, stirring frequently. Reduce the heat slightly and add the garlic, basil, oregano, pepper flakes, 1 teaspoon salt, tomato sauce, and water. Bring the sauce to a boil, stirring, then lower the heat to a simmer. Remove approximately 1½ cups of the sauce and store for another use.

5. Grate the mozzarella and set it aside.

6. Drain the potatoes. Brush the remaining 2 tablespoons of olive oil over the bottom and sides of a large deep baking pan (about 11 × 13 inches). Spread one third of the drained potatoes in a layer in the bottom of the pan and sprinkle them with salt and pepper to taste. Spread one third of the sauce over the potatoes, and top with one third of the grated mozzarella. Repeat with two more layers of potatoes, sauce, and cheese, using half the remaining ingredients for each layer. You should finish with the cheese.

7. Cover and bake the lasagna for 1 hour. Uncover and continue baking 40 to 60 mintues longer (check after 30 minutes), until the potatoes are tender and the top is golden brown.

Mango Chicken Breasts with Cardamom Sauce

YIELD: 4 SERVINGS

*D*on't be thrown off by the exotic-sounding combinations in this weekend dinner dish. The distinctive flavors work fantastically well together. If you can't find mango, papaya may be substituted with excellent results.

2 whole boneless chicken breasts
1 cup plain yogurt
1 teaspoon ground coriander
1 teaspoon powdered ginger
½ teaspoon turmeric
1 large, ripe mango
1 medium onion
2 tablespoons butter
½ teaspoon ground cinnamon
½ teaspoon ground cardamom
½ cup water

1. Cut each whole chicken breast in half. Trim the breast of fat and remove the tough white tendon running through the tenderloin. Place the chicken in a non-metal baking dish.

2. In a small bowl, mix the yogurt, coriander, ginger, and turmeric. Pour the sauce over the chicken breasts. Cover and refrigerate to marinate at least 2 hours, and preferably overnight. Make sure the chicken is completely coated, so that no meat will be exposed and dry out.

3. When ready to cook, preheat the oven to 400° F.

4. Peel the mango and cut it into ⅓-inch slices. Set aside on a plate. Cut the onion into ⅓-inch slices.

5. Place the butter in a small saucepan and melt over medium heat. Add the sliced onion and sauté, stirring, for 5 minutes. Add the cinnamon and cardamom and stir to coat. Add the water and bring the sauce to a boil. Remove from heat.

6. Remove the chicken breasts from the marinade and place them in an ungreased baking dish. (Do not scrape off any marinade that clings to them, but do not add any marinade left in the dish, either.)

7. Place a spoonful of sautéed onion over each chicken breast. Use all the onion and reserve any sauce that remains. Place the mango slices over the chicken and pour any juice that has drained onto the plate over the chicken. Cover the dish tightly with foil and bake 15 to 20 minutes.

8. When ready to serve, bring the remaining cinnamon-cardamom sauce to a boil and spoon it over the chicken.

Honey-Lemon Baked Salmon

YIELD: 4 SERVINGS

*F*or a while, it seemed like every salmon dish had to have something to do with dill. Nothing against dill, but what about trying salmon and something new? Say honey or lemon—or both?

1 teaspoon olive or vegetable oil for pan
½ tablespoon honey, orange blossom if available
2 tablespoons lemon juice
2 tablespoons orange juice
1½ pounds skinned salmon fillet (clean weight, not including skin)
1 lemon
Salt and freshly ground pepper to taste

1. Preheat the oven to 425° F.

2. Brush a jelly roll pan or other large flat ovenproof pan with the oil.

3. Mix the honey, lemon juice, and orange juice together in a small bowl.

4. Place the whole salmon fillet on the oiled pan. Brush the top of the fillet with the honey glaze. Bake for 8 to 10 minutes, or just until the salmon is cooked through and lightly browned.

5. Cut 4 thin slices from the lemon. Remove any seeds from the slices.

6. Remove the salmon from the oven and cut it into 4 serving portions. Place each portion on a heated plate and sprinkle with salt and pepper to taste. Place 1 lemon slice on each salmon piece. Serve immediately.

Steamed Lobster

*L*obster in the rough is the perfect summer weekend food. It's delicious and special, without being too formal (after all, you're eating it with your hands) and it can be served hot, with luscious drawn butter, or temptingly chilled. However it's served, we've always loved it—and we just learned a better way to cook it at home, by steaming instead of the traditional boiling method. The result is much like that of steaming vegetables—better texture, more flavor retained. Here's how.

1. Fill a large pot with ¼ to ½ inch of water. Cover the pot tightly, set it over high heat, and bring water to boil.

2. Remove cover, quickly place live lobster in the pot, and re-cover the pot.

3. Watch the lid. When the steam starts to escape from under the lid, look at the clock and start timing. It will take about 7 minutes for 1-pound lobsters; 1½-pounders will take 12 minutes; and 2-pounders will take 15.

Szechwan Lo Mein Salad with Spicy Peanut Sauce

YIELD: 6 TO 8 SERVINGS

A classically trained cook we know claims she will eat spicy peanut sauce on virtually anything—she specifically mentioned a Belgian waffle and a bowl of fresh cherries. For most of us, those combinations might be a bit hard to swallow, but spicy peanut sauce *is* delicious and exceedingly versatile, which may explain why recipes for it have been around Chinese kitchens for centuries. This is a tasty make-ahead dish that goes well with grilled chicken or flank steak. The spicy sauce keeps well in the refrigerator for later use as a marinade or for stir-frying.

SPICY PEANUT SAUCE:
3 large cloves garlic
2 teaspoons minced fresh ginger
¼ cup soy sauce
¼ cup water
¼ cup rice vinegar
1 tablespoon honey
4 drops Tabasco sauce, or to taste
2 tablespoons sesame oil
6 ounces creamy peanut butter

LO MEIN SALAD:
1 pound lo mein noodles
1 teaspoon salt for cooking water
1 large carrot
1 large stalk celery
2 scallions
1 medium red bell pepper
¼ pound daikon
¼ pound Chinese cabbage
2 tablespoons sesame oil
2 tablespoons peanut oil
¼ pound fresh snow peas
3 ounces bean sprouts

1. Peel and chop the garlic cloves and ginger. (They do not need to be finely minced.)

2. Place the chopped garlic and ginger in a blender with

the soy sauce, water, and vinegar. Blend to purée the garlic and ginger.

3. Add the honey, Tabasco, sesame oil, and peanut butter and blend until smooth. Pour the peanut sauce into a medium bowl and set aside.

4. Cook the lo mein noodles in a large pot of salted water according to package directions. Place another, smaller pot of water over high heat and bring to a boil.

5. While the noodles are cooking, peel and cut the carrot lengthwise into 2-inch julienne. Slice the celery on the bias, into ¼-inch slices. Slice the scallions on the bias. Cut the pepper into ¼-inch slices. Peel and julienne the daikon. Shred the Chinese cabbage thinly.

6. Place the cooked noodles in a large bowl. Sprinkle the sesame and peanut oil over the noodles and toss. Add all the cut vegetables to the noodles.

7. Trim the snow peas and blanch in the boiling water for 1 minute. Rinse under cold water, drain, and add to the noodles along with the bean sprouts.

8. Pour the peanut sauce over the noodle mixture. Toss everything together, mixing well to coat all the vegetables and noodles with the sauce. Serve at room temperature or chilled slightly, not cold.

Smoked Salad with Prickly Pears

YIELD: 4 SERVINGS

*P*rickly pears, sometimes known as cactus figs, are available in the exotic fruit section of almost any supermarket. The trouble is, most people never know what to make with them. This smoky, tropical salad is a way to try your hand at something new. And you have a beguiling choice between trout and turkey.

1 small clove garlic
2 scallions (green part only)
3 tablespoons heavy cream, chilled
4 tablespoons sour cream
4 tablespoons plain yogurt
3 tablespoons drained prepared horseradish
Salt and freshly ground pepper to taste
4 large red prickly pears
1 medium cucumber
12 large fresh spinach leaves
2 whole smoked trout (4 ounces each) or 8 ounces smoked turkey

1. Peel and mince the garlic clove. Cut the scallion greens on the bias into thin (¼-inch) slices. Set aside.

2. Pour the heavy cream into a small bowl. Whip it, using a whisk, just until it starts to mound.

3. In a separate small bowl, mix together the sour cream, yogurt, horseradish, salt, pepper, and minced garlic. Using a flat spoon, fold the whipped cream into the sour cream mixture. Set the dressing aside.

4. Peel the prickly pears and cut them lengthwise into quarters. Remove and discard the seeds. Cut the quarters lengthwise into strips. Peel the cucumber and quarter it lengthwise. Remove and discard the seeds. Cut the quarters crosswise into strips. Place the prickly pear and cucumber in a medium bowl.

5. Remove and discard the stems from the spinach leaves. Wash and dry the leaves.

6. Skin and bone the smoked trout and flake the meat, or cut the turkey into bite-sized cubes. Add the trout or turkey to the bowl with the pears and cucumber. Pour the dressing over the mixture and toss gently to coat thoroughly.

7. Arrange the spinach leaves on four plates. Mound a portion of the salad on top of the leaves. Garnish with the scallions and serve.

Sliced Potato and Onion Pie

YIELD: 4 TO 6 SERVINGS

We are always trying to think of new quick and easy ways to accompany casual classics like baked chicken or meatloaf. This dish, which dresses them up deliciously, comes all the way from the mountains of France, where it is a revered common man's meal. The preparation time is short, the results terrific. And leftovers go beautifully with fried eggs the next morning.

4 medium all-purpose potatoes, washed and unpeeled
1 medium onion
2½ tablespoons butter
Salt and freshly ground white pepper to taste
8 to 10 ounces chicken stock

1. Preheat the oven to 400° F.

2. Thinly slice the potatoes and the onion.

3. Rub a large ovenproof casserole dish with ½ tablespoon of the butter. Layer the sliced potatoes and onions, starting with potatoes, in the buttered dish. Between each layer, dot with the remaining butter and sprinkle with salt and white pepper to taste. The final casserole should be 1½ to 2 inches thick (if it's not, add more potato and onion), and the top layer should be a mixture of potato and onion.

4. Pour the chicken stock over all. Cover the dish with foil and bake for 25 to 30 minutes.

5. Remove the foil and continue to bake until the top is crunchy and the potatoes are tender when pierced with a knife, about another 15 minutes.

6. Serve hot directly from the casserole dish.

Yellow Beans with Roasted Pecan Dressing

YIELD: 6 SERVINGS

A quick side dish with lots of character. The pecans should be well toasted to bring out their rich flavor. The pecan dressing is excellent with green beans as well; we chose yellow simply for an interesting change.

1 cup shelled pecans
1 tablespoon sugar
Salt and freshly ground pepper to taste
¼ cup vegetable oil
6 tablespoons cider vinegar
1 pound fresh, preferably young yellow (wax) beans

1. Preheat the oven to 375° F.

2. Spread the pecans in a layer on a large ungreased baking sheet and toast them in the oven. Turn them with a metal spatula after 3 minutes. Remove them from the oven when brown (about 7 minutes, in total) and let cool.

3. Set aside ¼ cup of the toasted pecans to use as a garnish. Chop the remaining pecans coarsely. Place them in a small bowl and sprinkle with the sugar, salt, and pepper. Toss. Add the oil and vinegar, mix well, and set aside.

4. Bring a large pot of water to a boil. While the water is heating, trim the beans. Cook the beans by placing them in the boiling water for about 5 minutes, until they are tender. (The time will vary somewhat according to their size. They should be tender, but still firm and bright in color.)

5. Drain the beans and place them in a serving dish. Add the chopped pecans and toss well. Top with the reserved whole pecans and serve immediately.

SPRINGTIME'S PEAK PRODUCE

Look for these vegetables in May or June, when they're always at their finest:
♦ Arugula
♦ Asparagus
♦ Beet Greens
♦ Chives
♦ Fiddlehead Ferns
♦ Garlic
♦ Lemon Grass
♦ Peas
♦ Rhubarb
♦ Snap Beans
♦ Sorrel

Cream Cheese Apple Pie

YIELD: 1 (10-INCH) PIE

A memorable cream cheese crust embraces this guaranteed crowd pleaser. Serve it with whipped cream or vanilla ice cream, but don't dress it up too much—its beauty is in its simplicity. The contrast of colors between the sugared and unsugared apples is too pretty to cover up, too.

CRUST:
1 cup flour
½ teaspoon ground cinnamon
¼ teaspoon salt
3 ounces cream cheese
½ cup butter

FILLING:
7 large, firm-textured apples, such as Cortland or Granny Smith
½ cup firmly packed brown sugar
2 tablespoons lemon juice
3 tablespoons butter

1. To make the crust, mix together the flour, cinnamon, and salt in a large bowl. Using a pastry blender or two knives, cut the cream cheese and butter into the flour mixture, until it is of uniform texture. Press the dough together with a large fork, then turn it out onto a floured board and knead it briefly, just until it holds together.

2. Roll the dough out into a 13-inch circle. Dust the circle lightly with flour, then fold it carefully and lightly into quarters and transfer to a 10-inch ungreased pie plate. Unfold the dough gently and fit it into the pan. Crimp the edges, then place the pie pan in the refrigerator to chill while you prepare the filling.

3. Preheat the oven to 350° F.

4. To make the filling, peel, core, and cut the apples into ½-inch slices. Remove one third of the slices and set them aside. Place the remaining two thirds of the apple slices into a large bowl. Add the brown sugar and lemon juice and toss to coat.

5. Remove the piecrust from the refrigerator. Spoon the sugared apples evenly into the piecrust. Arrange the reserved (unsugared) apple slices in a concentric pattern over the sugared apples. Dot the surface with the butter and place the pie in the oven to bake for 1 hour, until it is golden brown and bubbling. Serve warm, topped with whipped cream or ice cream, or at room temperature.

Cherry-Meringue "Shortcake"

YIELD: 8 SERVINGS

When the meringue layers are sandwiched with whipped cream and topped with cherries, this dessert looks like a fantasy version of a strawberry shortcake. In the summer, we also like this cake with a variety of the season's berries.

MERINGUE:
4 egg whites
¼ teaspoon cream of tartar
Pinch of salt
1⅓ cups sugar
2 teaspoons white vinegar
1 teaspoon vanilla

FILLING:
½ cup slivered almonds
1 pound fresh cherries
¾ cup heavy cream, chilled

1. Preheat the oven to 325° F.

2. To make the meringue, place the egg whites in a large bowl and beat them until they are frothy. Add the cream of tartar and salt and continue to beat until the whites are firm, but not dry. Gradually add the sugar, beating well. Add the vinegar and vanilla and beat just to blend.

3. Spread the meringue into an ungreased 10-inch springform pan. Place it in the oven to bake for 1 hour, until dry throughout. Remove the pan from the oven and let the meringue cool in the pan.

4. Raise the oven temperature to 350° F.

5. To make the filling, spread the almonds in a layer on a small ungreased baking sheet. Toast them in the oven for 5 to 7 minutes, until lightly browned. Remove them from the oven and let them cool.

6. While the almonds are toasting, stem and pit the cherries. Place them in a large bowl.

7. Pour the cream into a large bowl and beat it until it is stiff.

8. When the meringue is cool, run a knife around the edge. Unlock and remove the sides of the pan. Using a sharp knife, carefully cut the meringue horizontally into halves. Remove the bottom of the pan.

9. Place the bottom layer of the meringue on a serving plate, cut-side up. Spread it with a thick layer of whipped cream, reserving enough to top each serving. Layer the cherries on top of the cream. Press the top layer of the meringue, cut-side down, onto the cherries. Using a sharp serrated bread knife, cut the shortcake into wedges. Top each serving with an additional dollop of whipped cream. Serve immediately.

Coconut-Baked Pears

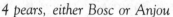

YIELD: 6 SERVINGS

Make sure to choose pears that are fresh and firm. A good fruity wine like Gewürztraminer best brings forth the flavor of the coconut and the hints of honey, lemon, and coriander. This dish is best served warm, with Pear Cream (see recipe below), but it is also delicious with ice cream or unsweetened cream.

4 pears, either Bosc or Anjou
2 cups cold water
1 tablespoon lemon juice
1½ tablespoon unsalted butter
8 ounces coconut macaroons
2 tablespoons honey
2 teaspoons ground cinnamon
1 teaspoon ground coriander
6 tablespoons fruity white wine, such as Gewürztraminer
½ teaspoon vanilla

PEAR CREAM (optional):
1 cup whipping cream, chilled
4 tablespoons confectioners' sugar
1 tablespoon pear brandy

1. Preheat the oven to 375° F.

2. Cut the pears in half, then peel and core them. Mix the water and the lemon juice in a medium bowl, and place the pear halves in the water to keep them from turning brown.

3. Rub the bottom and sides of a 9 × 13-inch ovenproof glass or ceramic baking dish with ½ tablespoon of the butter. Crumble the macaroons and sprinkle one-third of the crumbs in the bottom of the dish.

4. Drain the pear halves and arrange them neatly over the macaroon layer. Cover the pears with the remaining macaroon crumbs. (The pears should peek through.)

5. Cut the remaining 1 tablespoon butter into very small pieces and scatter them across the top of the pear-macaroon mixture. Drizzle with the honey, and sprinkle with the cinnamon and coriander.

6. Mix the wine and vanilla together in a small bowl and pour it over the pears.

7. Cover the pan with foil and bake for 30 to 40 minutes, until the pears feel tender when pierced with a knife.

8. If you are making the pear cream, pour the whipping cream into a large bowl and whip it just until it starts to mound. Add the sugar and pear brandy and mix just to blend. Refrigerate until you are ready to serve.

9. Uncover the baking dish, and broil the pears for 1 to 2 minutes until the coconut is well browned. Serve warm with a dollop of pear cream, ice cream or unsweetened cream on each serving.

Emma's Grand Marnier
Ice Cream

YIELD: 8 TO 10 SERVINGS

*T*his recipe came to us from a Bildner's customer who happens to be a parson's wife. She's known, among other things, for her "spirited" desserts. This one has a delightful creamy orange flavor that may remind you of those wonderful Creamsicles you ate so many of as a child. We like to make the dessert with homemade ice cream but in a pinch packaged ice cream will do (see the note below). It's almost sinful when served topped with Godiva Hot Fudge Sauce (see Index).

1¾ cups milk
5 egg yolks
⅔ cup sugar
¼ teaspoon salt
12 ounces frozen orange juice concentrate
2 teaspoons vanilla
1½ pints heavy cream
½ cup Grand Marnier

1. Pour the milk into a medium saucepan. Place over low heat until warmed.

2. Using a wooden spoon, mix the eggs, sugar, and salt in a separate medium saucepan. (Do not beat the eggs, or the custard will get foamy, making it difficult to monitor the cooking.) When the eggs and sugar are well blended, slowly whisk the warmed milk into the egg mixture.

3. Place the saucepan over medium heat and cook, stirring constantly with a wooden spoon, until the custard is thickened (about 5 minutes).

4. Remove the pan from the heat and strain the custard into a medium bowl. Whisk to cool slightly. Stir in the orange juice concentrate and the vanilla. Cover and refrigerate at least 1½ hours, and preferably overnight.

5. When you are ready to freeze the ice cream, mix the heavy cream and Grand Marnier into the orange custard. Place in an ice cream maker and proceed according to manufacturer's directions. Serve immediately or transfer to a container, cover tightly, and place in the freezer until serving time.

NOTE: *If time is critical, try this quick alternative—just soften a half-gallon of high-quality vanilla ice cream, mix in the orange juice concentrate and the Grand Marnier, and refreeze.*

Sorry, Bill, Chocolate Pudding

YIELD: 6 SERVINGS

S ome of us yearn for the good old days, when chocolate mousse was called chocolate pudding, and Bill Cosby had his own spy show. Is there still such a thing as a great pudding recipe that doesn't hail from a box? You bet there is, and here it is. With its double dose of chocolate, this creamy pudding will invariably invite comparison to the smoothest, richest chocolate mousse you've ever had. But don't get confused. This is pudding, pure and simple. We've dressed it up a bit by adding Meringue Stars and the Cocoa Cream (recipes follow), but a pudding purist can happily leave it plain.

2 tablespoons cornstarch
3 tablespoons unsweetened cocoa
3 tablespoons plus ¼ cup sugar
2 cups milk
¼ teaspoon salt
1 egg
2 egg yolks (save the whites for Meringue Stars, if desired)
⅔ cup semisweet chocolate chips
2 tablespoons butter
1½ teaspoons vanilla
Meringue Stars and Cocoa Cream (recipes follow) or lightly
   sweetened whipped cream for garnish (optional)

1. Sift the cornstarch and cocoa into a small bowl. Add 3 tablespoons of the sugar and stir to combine. Whisk in ¼ cup of the milk. Continue to whisk until the mixture is smooth.

2. Place the remaining 1¾ cups milk, the remaining ¼ cup sugar, and the salt in a medium saucepan over medium-high heat. Bring the milk mixture to a point just below the boil. Whisking constantly, add the cocoa mixture. Continue to whisk while you bring to a boil, then reduce the heat to low and simmer, stirring, until the cocoa mixture thickens, about 3 to 4 minutes. Remove the saucepan from the heat.

3. In a medium bowl, whisk the egg and egg yolks together. Gradually and slowly, whisking constantly, pour the hot cocoa mixture into the eggs. Then pour the entire mixture back into the saucepan and return it to the heat.

Cook, whisking, just until the pudding begins to boil (1 or 2 bubbles), about 2 minutes. Pour the pudding back into the bowl.

4. Add the chocolate chips and the butter to the pudding and stir to melt both. Stir in the vanilla and let the pudding cool to room temperature. Place it in a large serving dish or six individual serving dishes. Cover the pudding with plastic wrap or wax paper (press it down onto the surface if you don't want it to form a skin) and refrigerate until set, at least 1 hour. If desired, garnish with the Meringue Stars and Cocoa Cream (recipes follow) or lightly sweetened whipped cream.

Meringue Stars

2 egg whites (saved from Sorry, Bill, Chocolate Pudding)
¼ cup sugar
Butter for baking sheet (optional)

1. Preheat the oven to 275° F.

2. Place the egg whites in a large bowl and beat them just until soft peaks begin to form. Slowly and gradually add the sugar and continue to beat until the whites are firm but not dry.

3. Spoon the mixture into a pastry bag fitted with a star tip. Pipe the meringue onto a Teflon or lightly buttered baking sheet. Bake for 1 to 1½ hours, until dry. Set aside.

Cocoa Cream

¾ cup whipping cream, chilled
1 tablespoon cocoa
2 tablespoons sugar

1. In a large bowl, beat the cream until soft peaks begin to form. Sift the cocoa over the whipped cream, add the sugar, and continue beating the cream until stiff.

2. Spoon the whipped cream into a pastry bag fitted with a wide ribbon (plain) tip. Pipe the cream in a wide ribbon around the rim of the pudding. Top the ribbon of cream with a row of meringue stars (see above) and serve.

INDIVIDUAL PAVLOVAS

If you don't want to take the time to make rosettes of meringue for the chocolate pudding, or if you prefer to serve it with whipped cream, refrigerate and save the egg whites to make this light classic. We like to make it in individual portions because it's prettier to serve and just as easy.

2 egg whites
½ cup superfine sugar (or whirl ½ cup regular sugar in blender for 1 minute)
1 teaspoon cornstarch
1 teaspoon vinegar

1. Preheat the oven to 350°F. Mark 2 3-inch circles on a large sheet of parchment paper and set aside.

2. Place the egg whites in a medium bowl and beat until foamy.

3. Combine the sugar and cornstarch in a small bowl. While still beating the whites, add the sugar mixture one tablespoon at a time. Beat constantly for about five minutes, until almost stiff.

4. Add the vinegar and beat briefly.

5. Spread the meringue over each circle, building the sides up slightly higher than the middle. Place on a cookie sheet and bake for one hour, then turn the oven off and let dry overnight. Fill with whipped cream and fresh fruit.

TAKING the SHOW OUTSIDE

*A*n accomplished and rather adventuresome cook we know contends that the worst thing civilized man or woman ever did to a great dish of food was bring it indoors to serve it. Her idea of a perfect wedding reception is one where the bride and groom stir the coals and carve the roast pig right off the spit, where the revelers eat with their hands and then dance the night away. Granted, this vision may sound a bit extreme, but she steadfastly maintains that almost everything tastes better when served outdoors . . . something to do with the chemistry between the chaos of nature and the discipline of the refined palate.

Judging by the heavy volume of customers who flock to our stores almost every weekend, and on holidays specifically, seeking the perfect portable nibbles, we're convinced a whole lot of people agree with our friend. Basic fried chicken does taste just a wee bit exotic—and invariably more satisfying—when sampled with a crisp white Zinfandel on a leafy mountain overlook, or with spicy chips and gobs of potato salad and Bloody Marys from the tailgate of a Vista Cruiser before a homecoming football game.

Dining outdoors—a family spring picnic, a summer barbecue with neighbors, even a warm snack and a piping mug served to chums on a snowy chalet deck—is an eating experience that's often tucked away as one of life's more memorable interludes.

This chapter is made up of several outdoor menus just right for dining under the stars, or at the beach, or on the long road to the summer house. Often with an eye toward advance preparation, the menus contain sensible, imaginative, and verstaile food ideas that will please the crowd at everything from a steeplechase to a church picnic.

After all, as our adventuresome outdoor cooking friend would say, the world is merely an extended dining room.

Hot Grilled Littlenecks

YIELD: 6 SERVINGS

*F*or the first course of your dinner on the terrace, steam littlenecks in their own juice by heating them on the grill. The sauce is a spicy mayonnaise that is also great with shrimp.

1 egg
2 tablespoons lemon juice
Salt and freshly ground pepper to taste
½ cup olive oil
½ cup vegetable oil
2 medium shallots
1 large jalapeño pepper
¼ cup drained prepared horseradish
2 tablespoons clam juice, fresh or bottled
3 to 4 drops Tabasco sauce
3 tablespoons chopped fresh Italian parsley
2 tablespoons minced fresh chives
Crushed red pepper flakes to taste
3 dozen littleneck or cherrystone clams, in the shell

1. To make the mayonnaise, place the egg and 1 tablespoon of the lemon juice in a blender with salt and pepper to taste. Add ¼ cup of the olive oil and blend until smooth. Keep the blender running while you very gradually add the remaining ¼ cup olive oil and the vegetable oil. If you add the oil very gradually, the mixture will be creamy, and the oil will not separate. Place the mixture in a medium bowl and set aside.

2. Mince the shallots. Core, seed and mince the jalapeño. (Wear rubber gloves when working with jalapeño peppers to prevent irritation.)

3. Add the shallots and jalapeño to the mayonnaise. Add the horseradish, clam juice, Tabasco sauce, chopped parsley, and minced chives. Mix to blend.

4. Taste the mixture for seasoning and add crushed red pepper to taste. Refrigerate for at least 1 hour to let the flavors blend.

5. Prepare the coals or light the grill. Scrub the clamshells.

6. When the grill is hot, grill the clams until the shells open, for 5 to 10 minutes. Remove them from the heat as they open, trying to keep as much juice as possible in the shell. Keep checking and removing clams as they open. (If allowed to cook for too long, clams get rubbery.)

7. Open the clams all the way, place a dollop of sauce on each one, or pass with the sauce to dip, and serve immediately.

IN A CLAMSHELL

QUAHOGS

The Algonquin Indian name for a harshell clam found from the Arctic Ocean to Cape Hatteras. These East Coast clams are sold by size. The smallest are known as littlenecks, and the next larger size are cherrystones. In fact, the two are not different clams at all—the cherrystones are just a year or two older. Any quahogs larger (or older) than cherrystones are simply called chowder clams.

SOFTSHELL CLAMS

A tasty clam, ideal in size and texture for chowders, frying, or steaming. Also good on the half shell.

RAZOR CLAMS

The razor clam is not as popular as the quahog, partly because, with its sharp cutting edge and fragile shell, it is harder to harvest, so it is not as available. It's a little too tough to eat on the half shell, but the Eastern razors are good steamed, and all razors are good fried.

LITTLENECKS

No relation to the small quahogs, these clams are the most tender of the Pacific Coast clams. Two types of clams are classified as littlenecks— one that is native to California and one that was introduced from Japan. Both varieties are best eaten steamed.

COCKLES

Common (and beloved) in Europe, these clams are also found in the U.S., where the Pacific Coast varieties are the most tender. They are good in chowders, steamed, or fried.

GEODUCKS

A very large clam, which can grow to 8 inches long and weigh over 5 pounds. The meat is usually sliced and fried.

BUTTER CLAMS

A native delicacy from the West Coast. Small ones can be eaten on the half shell, but most butter clams are canned, and sometimes smoked.

Dry-Marinated Swordfish with Tomato-Lime Relish

YIELD: 4 TO 6 SERVINGS

*T*his recipe is similar to blackened fish in spices and preparation, only without the charcoal taste that sometimes results. Make sure to choose a thick steak so the fish stays juicy.

MARINADE:
2 teaspoons ground cumin
1 teaspoon sweet paprika
½ teaspoon dried thyme
½ teaspoon dried oregano
½ teaspoon cayenne pepper
½ teaspoon kosher salt

2 pounds fresh swordish steaks (at least 1 inch thick)

TOMATO-LIME RELISH:
1 large tomato
4 to 6 scallions (½ cup minced)
1 teaspoon minced jalapeño pepper (wear rubber gloves when working with jalapeños to prevent irritation)
1 teaspoon minced garlic clove
1 tablespoon minced fresh coriander
½ cup olive oil
3 tablespoons fresh lime juice
Salt to taste

1. Make the dry marinade by mixing together in a small bowl the cumin, paprika, thyme, oregano, cayenne pepper, and salt.

2. Rub the spice mixture into both sides of the swordfish steaks. Let them stand, covered, at room temperature for 30 minutes to 1 hour.

3. To make the relish, dice the tomato and mince the scallions. Mix them with the jalapeño pepper in a small bowl. Add the garlic and coriander and toss. Add the olive oil, lime juice, and salt and mix to blend. Set aside at room temperature until serving time.

4. Prepare the coals or light the grill; or if you are cooking this indoors, preheat the broiler.

5. Grill or broil the swordfish until it is cooked through, approximately 5 to 7 minutes on each side. Top each serving with some tomato-lime relish and serve immediately.

Orzo with Parsley and Garlic

YIELD: 6 TO 8 SERVINGS

With a hint of the Mediterranean, this simple side dish complements a variety of dishes—from grilled meat to lamb stew to coq au vin. It can be served either warm or at room temperature, but not chilled.

1 pound orzo (small, rice-shaped pasta available at most
*   supermarkets)*
Salt for cooking water plus ½ teaspoon
2 medium onions
4 cloves garlic
4 tablespoons butter
3 tablespoons chopped fresh Italian parsley
Freshly ground white pepper to taste

1. Cook the orzo in boiling salted water, according to package directions, until tender. Drain and place in a large bowl.

2. Meanwhile, finely dice the onions. Mince the garlic cloves finely.

3. Melt the butter in a medium sauté pan over medium-high heat. Sauté the onion in the melted butter for about 3 minutes, or until translucent. Add the minced garlic and continue to sauté, stirring occasionally, for another minute.

4. Add the onion-garlic mixture to the orzo. Sprinkle the parsley, ½ teaspoon salt, and white pepper over the mixture and toss well. Serve warm.

MORE TERRACE FOOD

Joan's Gazpacho

Flank Steak with Sesame-
Cilantro Marinade

Sautéed Scallops with Te-
quila and Lime

Fluffy Avocado Cream

Southwest Salad Bowl

YIELD: 4 TO 6 SERVINGS

*T*he colors of this salad bring to mind the Southwest—chili brown and burnt amber. But it's more than just a pretty plate. It makes a super weekend dish for hot weather, when just the idea of being in a steamy kitchen wilts the soul. We suggest you take the whole show outside, and grill some chicken on the barbecue to go with it or prepare our deck menu. Possibly add an icy pitcher of tart sangria or frozen Margaritas and a Santa Fe sunset.

DRESSING:
½ cup vegetable oil, preferably corn
⅓ cup plus 2 tablespoons fresh lime juice
1 teaspoon ground coriander
1½ teaspoons chili powder
½ teaspoon sweet paprika
½ teaspoon salt

SALAD:
1 large head romaine lettuce
2 medium tomatoes
1 ripe avocado
4 scallions
1 medium green bell pepper
1 small red bell pepper
½ cup pitted black olives
½ cup corn kernels, frozen and thawed

1. Combine all the dressing ingredients in a small bowl or blender. Blend or mix until smooth and set aside.

2. Tear the lettuce into bite-sized pieces, and place in a large bowl. Pour two thirds of the dressing over the lettuce and toss. Set aside.

3. Dice the tomatoes and avocado. Slice the scallions into ¼-inch pieces. Dice the peppers. Combine all the chopped ingredients in a large bowl, separate from the lettuce. Add the black olives and corn. Pour the remaining dressing over the vegetable mixture and toss.

4. Arrange beds of the dressed lettuce on individual salad plates and top with a mound of the vegetable mixture. Serve immediately.

American Bounty Cobbler

YIELD: 6 SERVINGS

*I*deally, this robust but cooling dessert should be served to complete a big spicy meal. Top the liberal amounts of native North American blueberries and cranberries with fresh cream, whipped cream, or ice cream for a look and taste born on the Fourth of July.

1 teaspoon butter for baking dish plus 6 tablespoons
2 cups cranberries, fresh or frozen
2 cups blueberries, fresh or frozen
1 tablespoon lemon juice
2 tablespoons Cassis
1 cup flour, unsifted
1 cup sugar
1 large egg
¼ teaspoon salt
Cream, whipped cream, or ice cream to top

1. Preheat the oven to 400° F.

2. Using 1 teaspoon of butter, grease a 10 × 6 × 2-inch baking dish.

3. Place the remaining 6 tablespoons of butter in a small saucepan and melt over moderate heat. Remove and set aside.

4. In a medium bowl, combine the cranberries and blueberries with the lemon juice and Cassis. Spread the berry mixture in a layer in the prepared dish.

5. In a medium bowl, combine the flour and sugar. In a small bowl, beat the egg until slightly frothy. Add the beaten egg and the salt to the flour mixture. Using a fork, mix the batter until it has the texture of coarse meal. (It will be somewhat crumbly.)

6. Spread the batter over the mixed berries. Drizzle the melted butter over the top.

7. Bake for 30 minutes, or until golden brown. Serve warm with cream, whipped cream, or ice cream.

BEACH FOOD

Certain foods are a perfect companion for beachcombing, while others just don't work at all. These are some of our—admittedly quirky—preferences:

WHAT TO PACK
breadsticks, popcorn, cold chicken or cold sliced steak, chilled lobster and shrimp salad, hard-boiled eggs, homemade shortbread cookies, pickles, hard sesame rolls, peaches and grapes, hot dogs and beer.

WHAT NOT TO PACK
bananas or strawberries, peanut butter, caviar, chocolate milk, red wine, apple cider, oranges, or chocolate chip cookies.

Steve's Guacamole Salsa

YIELD: 8 CUPS

*T*his most unusual appetizer is both a guacamole and salsa. We've found it to be a perfect dish to pack with tortilla chips for a picnic, and also excellent as a condiment served with grilled or broiled chicken or fish. It is the creation of Bildner's executive chef, Steve Petusevsky.

2 pounds avocados (about 3 to 4 medium)
2 medium tomatoes
1 small red onion
½ large red or yellow pepper
1 long, hot green pepper
3 large cloves garlic
2 tablespoons chopped fresh coriander
¼ cup olive oil
¼ cup fresh lime juice
Salt and freshly ground pepper to taste
Tabasco sauce to taste

1. Peel the avocados. Cut them in half, gently open, and remove the pits. Cut the avocados and tomatoes into ½-inch dice. Core and cut the tomatoes into ½-inch dice and place them in the bowl with the avocado. Finely dice the onion. Dice both the red pepper and the hot green pepper. Mince the garlic. Combine all the chopped vegetables in a large bowl.

2. Add the chopped coriander, olive oil, lime juice, salt, pepper, and Tabasco. Toss gently, being careful not to mash the avocados.

Baja Chicken

YIELD: 6 SERVINGS

*T*his is a simple, earthy, entree that tastes great served cold at a picnic or hot at an informal dinner party. On a picnic, we like to balance its crunchiness with soft, roasted eggplant, and pair its spicy flavor with slightly sweet coleslaw. Tangy lemon bars provide the perfect cooling finale.

1 clove garlic
1 small bunch fresh coriander
¼ cup olive oil
1½ teaspoons ground cumin
1 tablespoon chili powder
1 tablespoon sweet paprika
¼ to ½ teaspoon cayenne pepper
1 teaspoon dried oregano
1 lime
3 large, whole chicken breasts
½ cup lime juice

1. Preheat the oven to 375° F.

2. Mince the garlic clove. Remove the stems from the coriander leaves and discard. Chop the leaves. Combine the garlic and chopped coriander leaves in a small bowl. Add the olive oil and mix well.

3. Mix the cumin, chili powder, paprika, pepper, and oregano in a separate small bowl.

4. Cut the lime into 6 slices and set aside.

5. Place the chicken breasts on a large flat baking sheet. Brush the chicken breasts with the olive oil mixture. Sprinkle the spice mixture over the chicken. (The coating will be thick.)

6. Place a lime slice on each chicken breast and pour the lime juice over all. Bake for 30 to 40 minutes, until the coating is crunchy but not burned and the chicken is cooked through (juices should run clear when chicken is pierced with a knife or sharp fork).

MORE PICNIC DISHES

Spicy Peanut Chicken

Health Salad

Afternoon Apple Bars

Roasted Eggplant with Garlic and Lemon

YIELD: 6 SERVINGS

*H*ere is one of those rare dishes that is as good cold as it is hot. It makes a nice take-along lunch with cheese and crusty bread, and is equally at home served piping hot with grilled chicken or sirloin steak. To take it on a picnic, just pack it in an airtight container—but don't forget to pack the plates and forks, too.

2 pounds eggplant
½ cup olive oil
2 large cloves garlic
Juice of 1 lemon (about ⅓ cup)
½ teaspoon salt
Freshly ground pepper to taste

1. Preheat the oven to 425° F.

2. Cut the unpeeled eggplant irregularly into ½- to 1-inch pieces. Place the pieces in a large bowl with ¼ cup of the olive oil. Toss to coat. Spread the eggplant in a layer in an ungreased jelly roll or roasting pan. Place in the oven and roast until tender, about 20 minutes.

3. While the eggplant roasts, mince the garlic. Place it in a large bowl.

4. When the eggplant is cooked, remove it from the oven and add it to the garlic. Add the lemon juice, salt, pepper, and remaining ¼ cup olive oil. Mix to combine. Serve warm, chilled, or at room temperature.

Gold Rush Coleslaw

YIELD: 3 TO 4 QUARTS

A natural companion for a picnic, this colorful, zesty slaw is just the right accompaniment for Mexican-style chicken. It cools and tantalizes. We've also found it great on a sandwich of rare roast beef, pastrami, cold sliced chicken, or smoked duck.

1 (2½-pound) cabbage
¼ pound golden raisins
1 large clove garlic
8 ounces sour cream
2 tablespoons sugar
2 tablespoons cider vinegar
1 teaspoon curry powder
Salt and freshly ground pepper to taste

1. Remove the outer leaves from the cabbage. Trim, quarter, and core the cabbage. Cut each quarter into ¼-inch shreds. Place the shredded cabbage in a large bowl, add the raisins, and mix.

2. Mince the garlic clove. Place it in a small bowl. Add the sour cream, sugar, vinegar, curry, salt, and pepper and mix until smooth. Pour the sour cream dressing over the cabbage-raisin mixture and toss to coat. Let the coleslaw stand at room temperature for 30 minutes to marinate. After marinating, toss and serve immediately, or refrigerate until serving time.

Spicy Corn Bread

YIELD: 8 TO 10 SERVINGS

We've served this pepped-up variation of a Southwestern classic on a wide range of occasions—from a Super Bowl buffet to a child's christening party—to rave reviews. It's also a hearty accompaniment to chili or for a backyard barbecue, and it reheats well and easily.

4½ tablespoons butter
6 large jalapeño peppers, fresh or canned
1 small onion
6 ounces cheddar or Monterey Jack cheese (or half Cheddar, half Monterey Jack)
1½ cups cornmeal
½ cup whole-wheat flour
½ cup flour
2 teaspoons baking powder
½ teaspoon baking soda
1 teaspoon salt
1 tablespoon honey
2 eggs
¾ cup milk
1 16-ounce can cream-style corn

1. Preheat the oven to 400° F.

2. Grease a 9 × 13-inch baking pan with ½ tablespoon of the butter.

3. Melt the remaining 4 tablespoons butter in a small saucepan over medium heat. Set aside.

4. Core, seed, and chop the jalapeño peppers. (Wear rubber gloves when working with jalapeños to prevent irritation.) Grate the onion. Grate the cheese.

5. In a medium bowl, combine the cornmeal, flours, baking powder, baking soda, and salt. Make a well in the center of the mixture. Place the honey and eggs in the well and pour the milk, creamed corn, and melted butter over them. Stir to moisten thoroughly. (The batter may be slightly lumpy.)

6. Stir in the chopped jalapeños, grated onion, and ¾ cup of the grated cheese.

7. Pour the batter into the prepared pan and sprinkle the top with the remaining grated cheese. Bake for 25 to 30 minutes, until the top is golden and springs back when touched. Cool for 5 minutes, then cut and serve immediately or let the corn bread cool completely.

Lisa's Lemon-Butter Bars

YIELD: APPROXIMATELY 36 BARS

*T*hese bars have a firm shortbread crust and a very lemony filling, making them a perfect finish for a spicy meal like this Mexican picnic. We also love them with afternoon tea.

CRUST:
2 cups all-purpose flour
1 cup sugar
1 cup butter, well chilled

FILLING:
5 tablespoons butter
2/3 cup sugar
2/3 cup fresh lemon juice
4 eggs
2 tablespoons confectioners' sugar

1. Preheat the oven to 300° F.

2. To make the crust, place the flour, sugar, and butter in the bowl of a food processor fitted with a steel blade. Process just until the dough holds together. Press it evenly into an ungreased 9 × 13-inch pan, in one flat layer. Using a fork, poke holes over the entire surface, all the way through to the pan. Bake for 25 to 30 minutes, just until the edges begin to brown. Remove the pan from the oven.

3. Leave the oven on at 300° F.

4. To make the filling, while the crust is baking, melt the butter in a small saucepan over low heat.

5. Combine the sugar and lemon juice in a medium bowl. Whisk in the melted butter. Whisk in the eggs one at a time and continue to whisk just until the mixture is well blended.

6. Pour the filling over the partially baked crust. Bake for 15 minutes until the filling is set. Let cool for 1 hour, then dust with sifted confectioners' sugar and cut into bars.

Trombly's Peanut Butter Pâté

YIELD: ABOUT 1½ CUPS

Sometimes food is as interesting to discuss as it is to eat. A colorful vendor of ours, Trombly's Peanut Butter Fantasies, supplied this fascinating recipe for a pâté that is bound to excite great comment—and compliments—at your next cookout or tailgate party. Serve with plain crackers—dare we suggest ordinary Saltines?

2 slices bacon
3 scallions
3 medium fresh mushrooms
1 tablespoon butter
1 (8-ounce) package cream cheese, room temperature
2 tablespoons creamy peanut butter
2 tablespoons heavy cream
2 tablespoons lemon juice
¼ teaspoon salt
Freshly ground pepper to taste

1. Place the bacon in a small skillet over medium-high heat. Cook the bacon slices until crisp, then place on paper towels to drain. Do not rinse the skillet. When the bacon is cool, crumble and set aside.

2. Trim and cut the scallions into slices on the bias. Set aside.

3. Trim and chop the mushrooms into ⅓-inch pieces.

4. Pour excess bacon fat from the skillet you used to fry the bacon. Add the butter and melt it over medium heat. Add the chopped mushrooms and sauté until they are tender, about 3 to 5 minutes. Remove from the heat and set aside to cool.

5. In a large bowl, beat the cream cheese with a spoon until soft and creamy. Add the peanut butter, heavy cream, and lemon juice, and beat until smooth.

6. Add the reserved mushrooms with the salt and pepper. Stir to blend. Pack the pâté into a crock or bowl and chill for at least two hours, or until ready to serve.

7. When ready to serve, combine the scallions and crumbled bacon in a small bowl. Sprinkle the mixture over the top of the pate and serve with crackers.

PEANUT BUTTER FACTS

David Thibodeau, the young entrepreneur behind Trombly's Peanut Butter Fantasies, located in Boston's historic Fanueil Hall district, provided us with some interesting peanut butter facts:

♦ Americans consume 700 million pounds of peanut butter per year—more than three pounds per person.

♦ Peanut butter contains 11 of 13 essential mineral elements needed for human nutrition, including phosphorous, magnesium, copper, zinc, and iron. Peanut butter has no cholesterol.

♦ Peanut butter was used extensively by Dr. John Harvey Kellogg, the cereal magnate, for nutritional and therapeutic purposes at his Battle Creek Sanitarium, a health food retreat in Michigan.

♦ More than half of the peanuts consumed by Americans are eaten in the form of peanut butter.

Barley Soup with Shiitake Mushrooms and Dill

YIELD: 2 QUARTS

Unusual for its full flavor yet absence of meat, here's a winter soup your mother (even your earth mother) would approve of. Travels well in a thermos and in the company of a sandwich, and makes a warming start for a tailgate party. The barley needs to soak overnight, but the final result is worth every minute of advance planning.

1½ cups pearl barley
2 small carrots
2 medium stalks celery
1 medium onion
1 medium parsnip
4 ounces fresh shiitake mushrooms (or 1 to 2 ounces dried, soaked in warm water for 20 to 30 minutes and rinsed)
5 medium mushrooms
1½ quarts chicken stock
2 teaspoons peanut oil
¼ teaspoon dried thyme
¼ teaspoon dried marjoram
1 dried whole bay leaf
¼ cup chopped fresh dill
½ teaspoon salt
Freshly ground pepper to taste

1. The night before you make the soup, place the barley in a large bowl and cover it with water. Let it soak overnight.

2. Drain the barley in a colander and rinse it with fresh water. Return it to the bowl and set it aside.

3. Dice the carrots, celery, onion, and parsnip.

4. Slice the shiitake and the other mushrooms into ¼-inch slices and set aside.

MORE TAILGATE FARE

Rick and Susie's Day at the Beach

Mount of Olives Spread

Banana-Mocha Cupcakes

5. Pour the chicken stock into a pan and place it over low heat to warm.

6. Pour the peanut oil into a large stock or soup pot and place over medium-high heat. Add the diced carrots, celery, onions, and parnsip to the hot oil. Toss and sauté for 2 to 3 minutes. Add the warmed stock, barley, thyme, marjoram, and bay leaf. Bring the liquid to a boil, then lower the heat and simmer until the barley is nearly cooked, about 45 minutes. If the soup seems too thick, add additional stock or water to lighten. Add the mushroom slices and cook another 5 minutes.

7. Remove the soup from the heat and add the dill, salt, and pepper. Remove the bay leaf. Taste, correct seasoning if necessary, and serve.

American Sushi

YIELD: 2 DOZEN SLICES OF EACH TYPE

*I*f you're like us, you adore little sandwiches that come with big flavor. Don't be thrown by the oddball name—these bite-sized gems come in a variety of great Western tastes. Try your own fillings and combinations, too. Terrific for a tailgate munchy, and fun for party food, too.

Roast Beef and Asparagus with Horseradish Dressing

2 fresh asparagus spears
1 tablespoon heavy cream
1 tablespoon sour cream
1 tablespoon plain yogurt
1 tablespoon drained prepared horseradish
⅛ teaspoon grated lemon rind
Salt and freshly ground pepper to taste
1 (7-inch) pita
6 thin slices deli roast beef

1. Steam or blanch the asparagus spears until they are tender and bright green. Run them under cold water. Set them on paper towels to drain.

2. Pour the heavy cream into a small bowl and beat it with a whisk until soft peaks begin to form. In a separate small bowl, mix the sour cream, yogurt, horseradish, lemon rind, salt, and pepper. Fold the whipped cream into the sour cream mixture.

3. Split the pita into two flat circles and place them inside up on a large cutting board. Spread each circle liberally with the dressing. Arrange the beef slices in a layer over the dressing (3 to each circle) and sprinkle with salt and pepper to taste. Place one asparagus spear on each circle, against the edge of the side nearest you. Roll the pitas up tightly around the asparagus spears.

4. Place the rolls seam-side down and cut them into ¼-inch slices. Cover tightly with plastic wrap until ready to serve.

MORE AMERICAN SUSHI FILLINGS

- Fresh crabmeat, a touch of mayonnaise, and strips of red bell pepper.

- Cream cheese, lemon rind, dried figs, and toasted almonds

- Roast turkey slices with Gold Rush Coleslaw

- Mount of Olives Spread with feta cheese, shredded lettuce, and chopped marinated dried tomatoes.

- Smoked salmon with Horseradish Dressing and prickly pear.

Ham and Beans

These are best served warm, but you may also serve them at room temperature.

2 slices bacon
1 (7-inch) pita
6 tablespoons baked beans
2 large slices cooked ham (preferably sliced into 7-inch rounds and fairly thick, about ⅛-inch)

1. Preheat the oven to 350° F.

2. In a small skillet over high heat, cook the bacon until crisp. Drain on paper towels. When cool, crumble.

3. Split the pita into two flat circles and place them inside up on a large cutting board.

4. Mash the baked beans with a fork and spread them in an even layer on each round. Top each layer with a ham slice, and sprinkle with crumbled bacon.

5. Roll the pitas up tightly and place them seam-side down on the board. Cut the rolls into ¼-inch slices and arrange them on a baking sheet. Bake for about 5 minutes, until heated through.

Cream Cheese with Nuts and Raisins

These are also good unbroiled. Just wrap them tightly in plastic wrap until ready to serve.

3 tablespoons shelled pecans
2 tablespoons raisins
2 tablespoons heavy cream
2 ounces cream cheese, room temperature
½ teaspoon grated orange rind
1 (7-inch) pita

1. Preheat the oven to 350° F.

2. Spread the pecans on a small ungreased baking sheet and toast them in the oven for 5 to 7 minutes, until well browned. Let them cool slightly, then chop them coarsely.

3. Raise the oven temperature to broil.

4. Chop the raisins.

5. Pour the cream into a small bowl and whip it, using a whisk, until it starts to mound.

6. Beat the cream cheese with a spoon until it is soft and creamy. Mix in the pecans, raisins, and orange rind. Fold in the whipped cream.

7. Split the pita into two flat circles and place them inside up on a large cutting board. Spread each side liberally with the cream cheese mixture. Roll the pitas up tightly and place them seam-side down on the cutting board. Cut the rolls into ¼-inch slices and place them on an ungreased cookie sheet. Broil them for 1 minute, just to heat through. Serve immediately.

Harvard-Yale
Hot Buttered Rum Mix

YIELD: ENOUGH FOR 20 SERVINGS

*S*ome hearty tailgaters we know served this with smashing results one freezing afternoon prior to *the* annual Ivy League football game. The game turned out to be rather humdrum, but everyone was clamoring for the hot rum recipe. A hint: save any leftovers for the holidays and skating parties. Here's to the lads in crimson and blue . . .

½ cup (1 stick) butter, slightly softened
1 cup brown sugar
1 heaping teaspoon ground cinnamon
1 heaping teaspoon ground nutmeg
⅛ teaspoon ground allspice
¼ teaspoon powdered ginger
½ teaspoon angostura bitters (in the condiments section)

1. To make the mix, place the softened (but not melted) butter in a medium bowl. Add the brown sugar gradually, and cream the butter and the sugar together, mixing well. Mix in the spices and bitters. Store tightly covered in the refrigerator for up to several months, or use immediately.

2. To use the mix, stir 1 to 2 teaspoons of the butter-spice mix into 2 ounces of dark rum and 4 ounces boiling water for each serving.

Bildner's Famous Red Potato Salad

YIELD: 6 SERVINGS

*T*he quintessential picnic food, and our top-selling item at Bildner's. Since there's no mayonnaise in the dressing, it's a perfect outdoor food—no chance of spoiling in the sun.

1½ pounds medium new red potatoes
1 shallot
2 tablespoons Dijon mustard
1 tablespoon coarse mustard (with seeds), such as Pommery
¼ cup virgin olive oil
2 tablespoons red wine vinegar
2 tablespoons chopped fresh Italian parsley
Salt and freshly ground pepper to taste

1. Wash and boil the unpeeled potatoes until just tender (about 20 minutes). Drain and cool them completely. Cut into ½-inch slices. Place in a large serving bowl and set aside.

2. Mince the shallot finely.

3. In a small bowl, combine the mustards and olive oil. Add the red wine vinegar, minced shallot, chopped parsley, and salt and pepper. Mix to blend.

4. Pour the mustard mixture over the sliced potatoes and toss to coat. Serve or keep covered in the refrigerator. Return to room temperature before serving.

VIDEO VICTUALS

*T*here are a lot of social theorists around who say that television—and more recently video rental films—have had a revolutionary impact on modern lifestyles, including naturally, modern eating habits. Corroborating evidence is as close as our cash register receipts. So far, the single busiest day of take-out food sales for a Bildner's store was a Super Bowl Sunday several years ago, when we couldn't make enough Bildner's Santa Fe Chili, zesty chicken wings, and six-foot hero sandwiches to meet demand. Well, we haven't been caught short twice. When Super Bowl Sunday rolls around now, our chefs work double time to keep the nibbles coming. The same kind of consumer rush happens for the seventh game of the World Series, the Stanley Cup Playoffs, the NBA finals, and the Olympics. Another species of hungry TV watcher appears at our take-out counters whenever the Academy Awards, the Grammys, or a network premiere of a top-ten movie is on the tube.

The TV dinner today is far from those brick-hard, foil-wrapped delectations from the Ozzie and Harriet years, which always seemed to feature tasteless green peas and a Salisbury steak that could be used in a pinch for a hockey puck. People today want taste as well as convenience. Our chefs have spent a lot of time thinking about the tastebuds of the denizens of the video revolution. In this chapter you'll find hearty stews and easy-to-make-ahead ragouts, plus tempting munchies that can double as Sunday afternoon movie fare or hors d'oeuvres for your next backyard bash or office cocktail party.

So sit back and enjoy the show.

Casablanca Ragout with Sweet Corn and Bell Pepper

YIELD: 4 SERVINGS

*I*t's difficult to think of two more complementary flavors than bell pepper and shrimp, which are the starring ingredients in this stew. A video junkie we know loves to serve this with his favorite classic film, chilled white Zinfandel, and garlic cheese toast. Here's looking at an easy supper.

16 large raw, unpeeled shrimp
1 small onion
1 medium stalk celery
1 small red bell pepper
1 small green bell pepper
2 teaspoons peanut oil
1 cup corn kernels, fresh or frozen and thawed
1 cup bottled clam juice
Pinch of cayenne pepper
¼ teaspoon dried thyme
1 tablespoon cornstarch
2 tablespoons chopped fresh parsley

1. Fill a large pot with water. Place over high heat and bring to a boil. Add the shrimp and return to the boil for 3 to 5 minutes, until they turn pink. Remove the shells and devein them. Set aside.

2. Dice the onion, celery, and peppers.

3. In a large skillet, heat the oil over medium-high heat. Sauté the diced vegetables for about 5 minutes, until almost tender.

4. Add the corn to the skillet. Reserve 4 tablespoons of the clam juice, and pour the rest into the skillet. Add the cayenne pepper and thyme and bring the mixture to a boil.

5. In a small bowl, mix the cornstarch with the reserved clam juice.

6. Lower the heat under the skillet to medium and reduce the mixture to a simmer. Slowly add the cornstarch mixture to the simmering liquid in the skillet, stirring constantly. Raise the heat and bring the liquid back to a boil, stirring, to thicken.

7. Add the reserved shrimp and the parsley, and heat for 3 minutes, until warmed through. Taste for seasoning, and correct if necessary with cayenne pepper and salt. Serve immediately.

TASTY MOVIE TITLES

WHEN EATING IN

Guess Who's Coming to Dinner
The Thief Who Came to Dinner
Dinner at Eight
The Man Who Came to Dinner
Sunday Dinner with a Soldier
Breakfast for Two
Chicken Every Sunday
Come and Get It
My Dinner with André

WHEN EATING OUT

Alice's Restaurant
The Atomic Café
Separate Tables
If Only You Could Cook
Diner
Table for Five
Breakfast at Tiffany's
Tea for Two
Dinner at the Ritz
Who Is Killing the Great Chefs of Europe?

WHEN REALLY EATING OUT

Picnic at Hanging Rock
Clambake
The Onion Field
Porkchop Hill

A MISCELLANY OF TASTY TITLES

Bananas
Duck Soup
Bread and Chocolate
Candy
Wild Strawberries
A Taste of Honey
From Soup to Nuts
Prime Cut
Under the Yum-Yum Tree
The Bacon Grabbers
The Biscuit Eater
The Pumpkin Eater
Lorna Doone
The Fortune Cookie

South Pacific Shrimp

YIELD: 2 SERVINGS

*T*he tropical flavors of macadamia nuts and coconuts are sharply accented by hot wasabi marinade on these butterflied jumbo shrimp. They make a tempting VCR snack or light supper.

2 tablespoons wasabi powder (found in Japanese sections of
*   most supermarkets)*
2 tablespoons water
Oil for baking sheet
8 jumbo shrimp
¼ cup macadamia nuts
2 scant tablespoons coconut, preferably unsweetened
2 lemon wedges

1. Preheat the broiler.

2. Mix the wasabi and water in a small bowl. Cover the bowl and let the mixture stand for 10 minutes.

3. Brush a baking sheet with oil.

4. Remove the legs from the shrimp. Cut the shell lengthwise, where the legs were attached. Slit the shrimp lengthwise, without cutting through the outer shell in back. Press the shrimp open to butterfly.

5. Chop the macadamia nuts coarsely.

6. Brush the butterflied shrimp with the wasabi mixture. Place the shrimp on the prepared baking sheet. Sprinkle the chopped macadamia nuts and the coconut over the top of the shrimp.

7. Broil the shrimp 1 to 2 minutes. Serve hot with lemon wedges.

Louisiana Tenderloins

YIELD: 4 TO 6 SERVINGS

*H*ere's a simple recipe we sell a ton of in our stores. We serve it as finger food whenever we throw a grand opening bash, and customers everywhere love it. These Cajun nuggets can be frozen and reheated for TV movies or Monday night football games. To get the full flavor of the spicy breading, squeeze a wedge of fresh lime over each serving.

3 large cloves garlic
¼ pound firm-textured bread slices (approximately 5 slices)
¾ teaspoon dried oregano
¾ teaspoon ground cumin
½ teaspoon cayenne pepper
½ cup chopped fresh Italian parsley
2½ pounds boneless chicken breasts
2 eggs
1 cup flour
½ pound butter (1 cup, 2 sticks)
¼ cup olive oil
Salt and freshly ground pepper to taste
1 lime

1. Preheat the oven to 200° F.

2. Mince the garlic cloves and set them aside.

3. Remove the crusts from the bread. Dry them on an ungreased baking sheet in the preheated oven for 10 minutes. Place the bread slices in the bowl of a food processor fitted with a steel blade. Add the garlic, oregano, cumin, cayenne pepper, and parsley. Process to blend. Place in a small bowl and set aside.

4. Trim the chicken breasts of any fat or tendon. Cut each breast crosswise into three 2-inch-wide strips.

5. In a small bowl, beat the eggs well.

6. Spread the flour out on a large plate. Spread some of the bread crumb mixture over another plate. Pat the chicken strips into the flour, one piece at a time, turning to coat both sides. Shake off the excess flour. To get just a light coating of crumbs, lightly brush one side of the chicken with the beaten egg. Place the egg-washed side of the chicken into the bread crumbs; then brush the egg onto

---

WHAT MAKES GOOD VCR FOOD?

♦ Easy to eat in front of the tube. That means finger food or one-utensil meals.

♦ Something that can be made ahead and put in the oven while you watch the first part of a movie, or first half of the game.

♦ If it is intended to be a meal rather than a snack, the dish shouldn't require a lot of accompaniments.

the second side of the chicken. Turn that side over to coat with crumbs. Set the breaded chicken pieces on a wire rack while you bread the rest of the chicken.

7. In a large skillet, melt the butter with the oil over medium-high heat. Fry the chicken strips until they are golden brown on both sides (2 to 3 minutes for each side). (They may need to be done in batches to provide enough room in the pan.) When chicken is browned, remove to a platter and sprinkle with salt and pepper. Just before serving, cut the lime into wedges and squeeze the juice over the chicken strips.

New Age Steak and Cheese

YIELD: 4 SERVINGS

*I*t's risky business to tamper with a classic, but we wouldn't suggest this variation of the great Philly cheese-steak sandwich unless we'd come up with something really hot. The blue cheese, mascarpone, walnuts, and cognac marinade create the stuff halftime dreams are made of.

4 tablespoons cognac or Armagnac (approximately 1 small bottle or "nip")
1 tablespoon walnut oil
½ cup plus 2 tablespoons olive oil
Freshly ground pepper to taste
½ teaspoon dried thyme
1½ pounds sirloin steak trimmed of fat (weight after trimming)
1 large onion
6 ounces blue cheese (Stilton or Roquefort)
3½ ounces mascarpone (an Italian cream cheese found in Italian markets, most delis, and some supermarkets, or substitute regular cream cheese)
3 tablespoons butter
½ cup shelled walnuts
4 submarine or sandwich rolls
8 large radishes
Salt to taste

1. In a medium bowl, combine the cognac, walnut oil, ½ cup of the olive oil, pepper and thyme.

2. Cut the steak into thin slices. Add the slices to the bowl with the cognac marinade.

3. Cut the onion into ¼-inch slices. Add the slices to the marinade and toss to cover the meat and onions with the marinade. Cover and marinate in the refrigerator for 3 hours or overnight.

4. When you are ready to make the subs, preheat the oven to 375° F.

5. In the bowl of a food processor fitted with a steel blade, purée the blue cheese, mascarpone, butter, and walnuts until smooth.

6. Split the rolls into halves. Spread each side generously with the blue cheese butter. Place them, buttered-side up, on an ungreased baking sheet and toast them in the oven for 10 minutes, until lightly golden.

7. While the bread is toasting, slice the radishes thinly and set them aside.

8. Heat the remaining 2 tablespoons of olive oil in a large skillet over high heat. Pour off and discard the marinade from the beef and onion mixture and drain the beef and onions on paper towels. Add the beef and onions to the skillet and, stirring, quickly sear them in the hot oil. (Do this in two batches if the pan is not large enough.) When the meat is cooked through (1 to 2 minutes), season the meat and onions with salt. Pile a portion of the meat and onions onto 4 of the bread halves and sprinkle the sliced radishes over the top. Place the other 4 halves over the meat and press together gently. Serve immediately.

Chipped Chicken Wings

YIELD: 4 SERVINGS

*I*t's difficult to think of two more all-American video snacks than potato chips and chicken wings. It took a dedicated video junkie and devoted snack hound—our executive chef—to dream up a recipe that brings them together. The chips must be thoroughly crushed to gain the full crunchiness.

1 cup sour cream
⅓ cup chopped fresh chives
¼ teaspoon salt
Freshly ground pepper to taste
1 (7-ounce) bag extra crisp potato chips
12 chicken wings
1 tablespoon butter for pan

1. Preheat the oven to 375° F.

2. In a small bowl, mix together the sour cream, chopped chives, salt, and pepper.

3. Using either your hands or a rolling pin, crush the potato chips well. Place the crushed chips in a large bowl.

4. Cut off and discard the wingtips from the chicken wings. Lightly butter a jelly roll pan or baking sheet.

5. Using a pastry brush, brush a layer of sour cream mixture on both sides of the chicken wings. Roll the wings in the crushed potato chips and place them in a single layer on the buttered pan.

6. Place the pan in the oven and bake the wings until crispy, golden, and cooked through, about 45 minutes. Serve hot.

German Potato Soup with Bacon and Onion

YIELD: 8 SERVINGS

*T*his is a hearty soup, ideal for a winter weekend at home with a fire, a friend, and a favorite video movie. It doesn't require a lot of preparation, but it does need to simmer for a few hours.

6 slices lean bacon
1½ pounds Spanish onions (about 1½ large onions)
8 medium fresh mushrooms
4 large potatoes
3½ tablespoons flour
7 cups beef stock

2 egg yolks
1 cup sour cream
½ teaspoon salt
Freshly ground pepper to taste
2 tablespoons chopped fresh Italian parsley
2 tablespoons chopped fresh basil (or 2 teaspoons dried)

1. Cut the bacon into ½-inch dice. Dice the onion. Chop the mushrooms into ½-inch dice.

2. In a large, deep pot over low heat, sauté the bacon pieces, stirring occasionally, for 5 minutes.

3. Raise the heat to medium. Add the onion and mushrooms and sauté for 5 to 10 minutes, until soft.

4. Peel and slice the potatoes ¼-inch thick. Set aside.

5. Blend in the flour, stirring well. Cook for 3 minutes, stirring frequently.

6. Gradually add the beef stock, stirring constantly. Bring the liquid to a boil, continuing to stir.

7. Add the potatoes and reduce the heat to low. Cover and simmer the soup for 1 hour.

8. In a small bowl, blend the egg yolks with the sour cream. Stir ½ cup of the hot soup into the sour cream-egg yolk mixture to temper it. Add this mixture to the soup, stirring constantly. Cook the soup for 10 minutes, stirring often. Do not let the soup come to a boil. Remove from the stove for a minute or so, if necessary.

9. Season the soup with the salt, pepper, parsley, and basil. Serve immediately. Or refrigerate, then warm over medium-low heat before serving. Do not boil.

Great Food for Fast Lives

We read a lot these days about the hectic lives of working people—perhaps a little too much. Who needs to be reminded how a busy work schedule can undermine even the best intentions of eating well? The simple fact remains that, homemaker or CEO, we all have schedules to keep.

The chapters in this section will help make life in the fast lanes of the Commerce Club or the school car pool much more palatable. You'll discover quick and easy breakfasts, nourishing lunches-to-go, delightful make-ahead meals, haute cuisine in a half hour, and perfect afternoon pick-me-ups you can pack in a flash.

Complicated schedules demand simple answers. Distinctive meal planning is often the first victim of the daily grind, but with just a bit of good planning and proper execution—combined with some great fast and easy recipes—you'll be on the road to eating and living well.

*O*ne of the busiest times of the day at a Bildner's store is early morning, when the smell of fresh-baked muffins mingles with the scents of cinnamon rolls and just-brewed coffee. Grabbing a quick bite of breakfast is certainly America's thing, which is one reason we work so hard to make the breakfast hour so appealing at our stores.

Breakfast should be something special, even if it's taken on the mad dash. Besides providing basic good nutrition, it can go a long way in helping to establish the tone and pace of a day's activities. As your mother always said, never skimp on breakfast.

This chapter is dedicated to the quick and nourishing getaway, with recipes that offer a high-energy yield and terrific taste. You may have seen the last of your bran flakes for a while.

High-Stress Shake

YIELD: 1 SERVING

*T*his is an ideal breakfast shake for a high-stress day not only because it's high in protein, calcium, and potassium, but also because its cool, creamy texture makes it a soothing start.

1 ripe banana
2 tablespoons creamy peanut butter
3 tablespoons non-fat dried milk
1 tablespoon honey, preferably orange blossom
½ cup honey-vanilla yogurt
½ cup ice cubes

1. Break the banana into halves or thirds and place it in a blender.

2. Add the peanut butter, dried milk, honey, yogurt, and ice cubes. Blend at high speed until all the ice is crushed and the shake is of uniform consistency. Serve immediately.

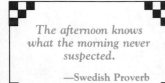

The afternoon knows what the morning never suspected.

—Swedish Proverb

Runner's Shake

YIELD: 1 SERVING

*O*ne of the reasons that this shake makes a good run-ner's breakfast is that it contains no dairy products or fat, making it easy to digest just after a run. It's also a nutri-tional and delicious beginning for those of us not off to such a running start.

1 tablespoon wheat germ
1 medium peach
¼ block tofu
½ cup ice cubes
¼ cup cold water
½ teaspoon ground cinnamon
1 tablespoon frozen lemonade concentrate

1. Preheat the oven to 350° F. Spread the wheat germ on a small ungreased baking sheet. Toast it in the oven for 1 to 2 minutes, just until lightly browned.

2. Peel the peach and cut it into quarters.

3. Place the tofu in a blender. Add the toasted wheat germ, ice cubes, and cold water to the tofu. Add the peach quarters (along with any juice that may have drained onto the cutting board as you cut the peach), cinnamon, and lemonade concentrate.

4. Blend at high speed until all the ice is crushed and the shake is of uniform consistency. Serve immediately.

Bildner Benedict

YIELD: 2 SERVINGS

A savory breakfast dish that can be made in a snap, the recipe is written for two but can easily be doubled or tripled. The important thing is to choose a full-flavored bread. It's a terrific way to feed a hungry group.

4 large eggs
½ teaspoon Worcestershire sauce
Salt and freshly ground pepper to taste
2 slices (1 inch thick) savory bread, such as cheese, onion, herb, or pepperoni and cheese
1 tablespoon butter

1. In a wide, shallow bowl or dish, beat 2 of the eggs lightly. Add the Worcestershire sauce, salt, and pepper, and beat until well blended and slightly fluffy.

2. Dip the bread slices into the egg mixture and let the liquid soak into the bread. Turn to cover both sides.

3. In a large skillet, heat the butter over medium heat. Add the bread slices and brown well. Turn the bread slices to fry the second side, then break the remaining 2 eggs into the pan and fry them next to the bread slices, sunny-side up or over-easy as you choose.

4. To serve, place the eggs on top of the bread slices, and sprinkle with additional salt and pepper to taste. Serve immediately.

OVER COFFEE

During the late 1600s, coffee prices reached $48 per pound in Britain—and it was still the most popular beverage.

In Turkey, a wife was once permitted to divorce her husband for failing to keep the family coffeepot filled.

According to legend, coffee's energizing powers were discovered when a ninth-century Ethiopian goatherd watched his flock grow frisky after eating the wild coffee cherries.

Egg and Toasted Almonds on Black Bread

YIELD: 2 TO 4 SERVINGS (THEY ARE QUITE FILLING)

*T*his quick breakfast getaway is a variation of the old bacon and egg sandwich. We've dropped the bacon and added the toasted almonds. A simple mix of boiled eggs, butter, salt and pepper, and toasted almonds is spread richly on a piece of toasted pumpernickel, or piled between two pieces to make a great commuter sandwich. As they say in the coffee-maker commercial, life is complicated enough at 7 A.M.

½ cup slivered almonds
4 eggs
4 or 8 slices pumpernickel bread (see note)
2 tablespoons butter
Salt and freshly ground pepper to taste

NOTE: *Use 4 slices if you are making a spread to top one piece of toast, 8 slices for commuter sandwiches.*

1. Preheat the oven to 350° F.

2. Spread the almonds in a layer on a small ungreased baking sheet and toast them in the oven for 7 minutes, until browned. Cool slightly, then chop and set aside.

3. While the almonds are toasting, boil the eggs for 3 to 4 minutes (for soft boil).

4. While the eggs are boiling, toast the pumpernickel, if you are spreading the eggs on toast rather than making a sandwich.

5. When the eggs are cooked, run them under cold water, then drain them and let them stand until they are cool enough to handle. Split the eggs open and scoop them into a bowl. Add the butter, salt and pepper, and the chopped almonds. Mix well, until the butter is melted, then spread the egg mixture on the toast. Serve immediately.

Make-Ahead Morning Muffins

YIELD: ABOUT 1½ DOZEN MUFFINS

*T*he batter in this recipe will keep in the refrigerator for up to a week, so it's possible for you to make fresh muffins every morning with a minimum of hassle. The batter can also be used to make fast and healthy pancakes.

1 cup boiling water
1 cup whole-grain cereal, such as Nutri-Grain or All-Bran
½ cup butter
¼ cup honey
½ cup brown sugar, lightly packed
½ cup white sugar
2 large eggs
1 cup buttermilk
1 cup milk
2½ cups flour
2½ teaspoons baking soda
2 cups raisin bran or raisin wheat flakes cereal
1 teaspoon salt
Oil or muffin papers for muffin tin

1. In a small bowl, pour the boiling water over the whole-grain cereal. Let the mixture stand 5 minutes to cool.

2. Place the butter in a large saucepan and melt over medium-high heat. Add the honey, brown sugar, and white sugar. Stir to combine and dissolve the sugars.

3. Remove the saucepan from the heat and beat in the eggs one at a time, beating well after each. Whisk the buttermilk and the milk into the butter mixture until well blended. Add the wet cereal mixture and stir to combine.

4. In a separate large bowl, mix the flour with the baking soda. Add the raisin cereal and salt and mix to combine.

5. Pour the liquid mixture onto the dry mixture and stir to blend. (Don't worry if it seems thin—it will thicken as it stands.)

6. Pour the muffin mix into an airtight container and store in the refrigerator. It will keep up to 1 week.

7. When ready to bake, preheat the oven to 400° F.

The critical period in matrimony is breakfast time.

—Sir Alan Patrick Herbert
Uncommon Law (1935)

8. Spoon mixture three quarters full into greased or paper-lined muffin tin. (Do not stir the batter when you take it out of the refrigerator, or it will make the muffins tough. Just spoon out what you need, re-cover the container, and return it to the refrigerator.)

9. Fill any empty spaces in the muffin tin with water. Bake for 20 minutes, or until a skewer inserted in the center comes out clean and dry. Serve immediately.

Lemon Pear Bread

YIELD: 1 (8-INCH) LOAF

*O*ur recipe tester found this quick breakfast recipe "delightful with tea and sautéed ham slices." Others we know swear that once you try it sliced and toasted in the morning, spread with cream cheese and lemon curd, you'll never settle for cheese danish again. It's easy to make it the night before.

½ cup glacéed pears, if available (see note)
2 large Comice or Anjou pears
⅓ cup butter plus ½ tablespoon for pan
½ cup lightly packed brown sugar
½ cup sugar
2 eggs
3 tablespoons vegetable oil
¼ cup sour cream
1 teaspoon lemon juice
2 cups flour
1 teaspoon baking soda
½ teaspoon ground cinnamon
½ teaspoon salt
1 teaspoon grated lemon rind
Equal parts cream cheese and lemon curd, softened to spread

NOTE: *Glacéed pears can be found in many specialty markets. If they are not available, do not substitute dried pears, just omit.*

1. Preheat the oven to 350° F.

2. If you are using them, chop the glacéed pears and set them aside.

3. Chop the pears. (Leave the skins on.)

4. Melt ⅓ cup of the butter in a small saucepan over medium heat. Grease an 8¼ × 4½-inch loaf pan with the remaining ½ tablespoon of butter.

5. Place the brown sugar and the white sugar in a medium bowl. Stir in the melted butter. Beat in the eggs. Add the vegetable oil, sour cream, and lemon juice, and mix well.

6. Sift the flour, baking soda, cinnamon, and salt together over the batter. Stir the flour mixture into the batter. Add the reserved chopped fresh pears and the grated lemon rind. Mix just to combine.

7. Pour the batter into the buttered loaf pan. Sprinkle the top with the chopped glacéed pears, if you are using them, and press them into the batter slightly. Bake for approximately 1 hour, until a skewer inserted in the center of the loaf comes out clean and dry.

8. To serve for a fast breakfast, slice and toast the bread. Spread the toasted slices with a mixture of equal parts softened cream cheese and lemon curd.

Vanilla-Eggnog Custard Sauce

YIELD: APPROXIMATELY 3 CUPS

*H*ere's a grand fresh start idea—a lovely sauce that goes great on fruit. It's not too sweet, as the flavor comes mostly from the vanilla bean. Besides being a quick breakfast, it's a soothing late night snack. It will keep just fine for up to three days in the refrigerator, which means you can make it on a weekend to start off the long week ahead. We've made some fruit suggestions, but you can use it with any combination of fruit—even canned fruit tastes good with it.

1 whole vanilla bean
2 cups milk
4 egg yolks
¼ cup sugar
Pinch of salt

1. Split the vanilla bean lengthwise and place it in a small saucepan. Pour in the milk. Over high heat, bring the milk to a point just below the boil; then remove the pan from the heat, cover it, and let it steep for 45 minutes.

2. After 45 minutes, reheat the milk. Place the egg yolks and sugar in a medium bowl and whisk to blend. Slowly and gradually add the hot milk to the egg yolk mixture, whisking constantly. When all the milk has been whisked in, return the mixture to the saucepan. Heat, stirring constantly, until the custard is thick enough to coat the back of a spoon.

3. Remove the saucepan from the heat and strain the custard through a sieve into a medium bowl. Scrape the seeds from the vanilla bean and add them to the custard. (Discard the pod.) Let the custard cool to room temperature, then cover it and refrigerate. It will keep for up to 3 days.

4. Serve cold over fresh fruit. For example:
• sliced bananas and seedless orange sections
• mixed raspberries, blackberries, and blueberries
• pears with toasted walnuts
• papaya slices, sliced kiwi, and cubed melon
• pitted cherries and sliced peaches

FAVORITE FAST STARTS

♦ Vanilla yogurt with Mother's Warm Applesauce, hot spiced-apple herb tea

♦ Cream of Wheat with brown sugar, cinnamon, and cream; cappuccino

♦ Cinnamon toast; hot, lemony tea

♦ Oatmeal with stewed apples and raisins, hot cider

♦ Peanut butter and banana on toasted English muffins, hot coffee

♦ Cold leftover pizza and a big glass of milk

A government study found that at least a third of the
American work force eats lunch within a few feet of where
they work—in other words at their desks, workbenches, or
over by the office water cooler. We've all heard stories
about extravagant three-martini marathons, but the fact is
that to most of us, whether college students or busy ac-
count executives, lunchtime is by necessity a rather func-
tional and often drab affair involving whatever can be
hastily tossed together at the day's beginning, grabbed
from a stack of shrink-wrapped deli sandwiches, or coaxed
from a vending machine.

Alas, there seems to be a sizable dose of Calvinist guilt
involved with the American lunching ethic—the best
lunch of all is one where we not only get a tidy bounce of
brown bag nourishment, but also get some paperwork done.

THE BEST SANDWICHES

♦ Grilled eggplant, buffalo
mozzarella, and sliced
red onion with a dab of
extra-virgin olive oil on a
baguette

♦ Peanut butter, sliced
banana, and Shaker apple
butter on toasted
anadama or cornmeal
molasses bread

♦ Brie with a tomato slice
broiled on a garlic bagel
spread with Dijon
mustard

♦ Roats turkey with Boursin
cheese and shredded
lettuce on a whole
wheat pita

♦ Roast beef with English
or Farmhouse Cheddar
and grilled onions on
light rye.

♦ Smoked ham with Bel
Paese and apple slices on
oatmeal bread

♦ Neufchâtel and orange
marmalade with chopped
dates on whole wheat

It's too bad we didn't learn the proper role of the noontime meal from our European ancestors, who lavished time and energy on its preparation and eating.

A woman executive we know loves to spend her lunch hour out window shopping. Yet she never short changes lunch. The lunch she brings from home is suited to her perambulations: homemade spring rolls wrapped in convenient wax paper and dispatched as easily as a Fifth Avenue hot dog: nifty little containers of custom-blended fruit and yogurt and other healthy things; cool and tempting salads; small gourmet sandwiches; and dessert bars.

This woman is by profession an efficiency expert—and she tells us that a little bit of advance planning and creative packaging are the secrets of a good lunch on the go. For these recipes our chefs put their minds to the possibilities of executive brown bags, kid-pleasing lunches, and afternoon pick-me-ups.

Lunch on the run may have never had it so good.

Joan's Gazpacho

YIELD: 8 SERVINGS

*T*his zesty lunch-to-go recipe was originally supplied by Joan Bildner, Jim's mother. It's an easy blender recipe. (We chop the onion by hand, however, to avoid the slightly bitter taste that results from the extracted juice when onions are puréed.) This is a light and low-calorie lunch to pack in a thermos. Take along croutons and chopped fresh parsley to garnish.

1 large onion
1 medium pepper, any color
1 medium cucumber
4 large cloves garlic
8 whole canned Italian tomatoes, drained (about half of a
*   2-pound can)*
1 quart tomato juice
¼ cup olive oil
¼ cup red wine vinegar
Tabasco sauce to taste
Freshly ground pepper to taste
1½ teaspoons salt
¼ cup chopped fresh Italian parsley and croutons for garnish

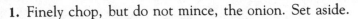

1. Finely chop, but do not mince, the onion. Set aside.

2. Coarsely chop the pepper, cucumber, and garlic.

3. Put half the pepper, cucumber, garlic, and tomatoes in a blender. Add half the tomato juice, olive oil, and vinegar. Blend just until the vegetables are medium chopped, but thoroughly blended. They should be neither too chunky, nor puréed. Transfer the vegetables to a large bowl.

4. Place the remaining half of the pepper, cucumber, garlic, and tomatoes in the blender. Add the remaining tomato juice, olive oil, and vinegar, and blend as before. Add to the bowl with the first half.

5. Stir in the reserved chopped onion, Tabasco, black pepper, and salt. Chill until ready to serve or pack in a thermos and chill.

6. When ready to serve, sprinkle each serving with chopped parsley and pass the croutons. If you are packing the gazpacho for lunch, place the parsley and croutons in sandwich bags and garnish just before eating.

MICROWAVE LEFTOVERS

Here are some dinner recipes that make great lunches to pack along in a Tupperware container and reheat: Christmas Enchiladas, Cross-Country Baked Potatoes, Pasta Salad with Shrimp and Pine Nuts, Spicy Peanut Chicken, Cajun Meatloaf, Irish Lasagna.

Italian Tuna Salad

YIELD: 8 TO 12 SERVINGS

This lunch-to-go is a nice variation on tuna-macaroni-mayonnaise salad. You can substitute canned white beans for convenience sake, but the dried beans lend the salad a firmer, more appealing texture.

1½ cups dried white beans (or 2 [16-ounce] cans)
1 medium green bell pepper
1 small red onion
1 large bulb fennel
½ cup olive oil
¼ cup red wine vinegar
Salt and freshly ground pepper to taste
12 ounces tuna, packed in olive oil (see note)
¼ cup chopped fresh fennel greens, if available
12 pitted black olives for garnish

NOTE: Tuna packed in olive oil can be found in the imported foods section of most supermarkets.

1. Place the dried beans in a large pot. Cover the beans with water. Bring the water to a boil over high heat. Cover the pot, remove it from the heat, and let stand 1 hour. After 1 hour, drain the beans and cover them with fresh water. Return the pot to the heat and bring it back to the boil. Lower the heat and simmer the beans, covered, for 30 to 45 minutes, until tender. If you are using canned beans instead, simply drain and rinse them.

2. While the beans are cooking, cut the pepper into ¼-inch julienne. Dice the red onion. Trim the fennel bulb, cut it lengthwise into quarters, and remove the core. Cut it crosswise into ¼-inch slices. Place the pepper, onion, and fennel together in a large bowl.

3. Add the drained beans to the bowl. Add the olive oil, vinegar, salt and pepper. Toss to coat.

4. Drain and flake the tuna and add it and the chopped fennel greens (if available).

5. Toss well. Garnish with the pitted black olives. Serve immediately or refrigerate.

Health Salad

YIELD: 6 TO 8 SERVINGS

*O*ur executive chef at Bildner's is a bit of a health nut—although lovable—so he created a sumptuous salad in his own image. The kasha, a buckwheat groat, can be easily found at health food stores and many supermarkets; we like to use it in salads because it holds the dressing so well and has a nice woodsy flavor. This salad travels well. Pack it for a deliciously healthy lunch, and avoid the long lines at the deli.

DRESSING:
½ cup orange juice
1 cup olive oil
Salt and freshly ground pepper to taste
2 tablespoons balsamic vinegar (see note)

SALAD:
1 pound onions (about 4 medium)
3 tablespoons peanut oil
Salt to taste plus 2 teaspoons for cooking water
Freshly ground pepper to taste
2 medium bunches fresh watercress
1 pound large bowtie noodles
½ pound kasha

NOTE: *Balsamic vinegar is also called* aceto balsamico—*available in specialty and Italian markets, as well as some supermarkets.*

1. Combine all dressing ingredients in a blender and blend until smooth. Let the dressing rest in the blender while you assemble the salad.

2. Dice the onions.

3. In a large sauté pan, heat the peanut oil over medium heat. Place the diced onion in the pan, sprinkle with salt and pepper to taste, and sauté, stirring often, for about 20 minutes. (The onion should brown but not burn.)

4. Rinse the watercress well and pat it dry. Cut the stems off below the second set of leaves.

5. Cook the noodles and the kasha separately, in two large pots of salted water, according to their package directions. Drain both and combine them in a large bowl.

THE MEXICAN MICROWAVE LUNCH

Here's a great way to take advantage of the newest piece of standard office equipment:

1. Spread the inside of a pita pocket with refried beans, salsa, and grated Cheddar or Monterey Jack cheese. Wrap it in plastic and pack a separate sandwich bag of shredded lettuce, chopped tomato, and diced red onion.

2. At lunchtime, microwave the pita until the cheese is melted. Open it and fill with chopped veggies.

6. Reblend the dressing briefly. Pour the dressing over the noodle-kasha mixture and toss to coat. (The salad can be made ahead up to this point and stored in the refrigerator.)

7. Add the onions and watercress to the noodle-kasha mixture and toss to mix thoroughly. Serve at room temperature.

Fluffy Horseradish Dressing

YIELD: APPROXIMATELY 1¼ CUPS

*T*his whipped dressing is delicious spread on roast beef sandwiches, tossed in salads, or served with roast tenderloin. Since no eggs are used, the dressing will keep in the refrigerator for several days and is great to take along to a picnic or tailgate party.

¼ cup butter
½ cup heavy cream, chilled
2 tablespoons drained prepared horseradish
1 tablespoon lemon juice
Salt to taste
Freshly ground white pepper to taste

1. Melt the butter in a small saucepan over low heat.

2. Pour the cream into a medium bowl and beat it just until it begins to get stiff.

3. Mix the horseradish, lemon juice, salt, and white pepper together in a small bowl. Whisk the melted butter into the horseradish mixture in a slow, steady stream.

4. Using a spatula or flat spoon, fold the whipped cream into the dressing. Use immediately or store, covered, in the refrigerator until serving time.

Banana-Mocha Cupcakes

YIELD: 12 MUFFINS

We developed this engaging cupcake recipe from a chocolate-banana cake we were served by Susan Peery, the food editor of *Yankee* Magazine. Susan sent the recipe along with the kind suggestion that we try something new with it. It seemed to us that banana-mocha cupcakes would make a spectacular afternoon pick-me-up, a great lunch box stuffer, or simply a new morning muffin. They're wonderful with coffee or hot chocolate.

Oil or 12 muffin papers for muffin tin
2 large, ripe bananas
2 tablespoons instant espresso powder
½ cup milk
9 tablespoons (1 stick plus 1 tablespoon) butter, softened
1¼ cups sugar
¼ teaspoon salt
2 eggs
1 cup flour
½ cup unsweetened cocoa

1. Preheat the oven to 400° F.

2. Lightly brush the muffin tin with oil, or line it with muffin papers.

3. Place the peeled bananas in a small bowl. Using a fork, mash them well and set them aside.

4. Place the instant espresso in a separate small bowl. Stir in the milk and let the espresso dissolve.

5. Place the softened butter in a medium bowl with the sugar and salt. Beat with a wooden spoon or electric mixer until creamy. Add the eggs and beat until fluffy. Add the mashed bananas and the milk-coffee mixture and beat well.

6. Sift the flour and cocoa onto the batter. Mix quickly just until the dry ingredients are incorporated into the batter.

7. Pour the batter into the prepared muffin tin. Each cup should be about three quarters full. Bake for 20 to 30 minutes, until a skewer inserted in the center of the muffins comes out clean and dry. Let cool for 5 to 10 minutes in the tins, then turn the muffins out onto a rack to cool completely.

Afternoon Apple Bars

YIELD: 16 BARS

*F*ennel sugar adds an unexpected flavor to these dressy afternoon snack bars. They are extremely easy to make, with little clean-up. A terrific lunch-to-go dessert, or an afternoon pick-me-up with a cup of hot tea or fresh coffee at your desk, with your secretary holding your calls for a few meditative moments.

1 teaspoon fennel seeds
½ cup white sugar
½ tablespoon butter for baking pan plus ¼ cup
2 large, tart apples, such as Granny Smith
½ cup brown sugar, lightly packed
1 egg
1½ teaspoons vanilla
1 cup flour
1 teaspoon baking powder
¼ teaspoon salt
½ teaspoon ground cinnamon

1. Preheat the oven to 350° F.

2. Place the fennel seeds and sugar together in a blender and blend at high speed to crush the seeds (see note).

3. Using ½ tablespoon of the butter, grease a 9 × 9-inch baking pan.

4. Melt the remaining ¼ cup butter in a medium saucepan over medium heat.

5. While the butter melts, peel, core, and dice the apples.

6. Remove the saucepan from the heat. Add the fennel sugar and the brown sugar to the butter and mix well. Add the egg and vanilla and blend quickly but thoroughly.

7. Sift the flour with the baking powder, salt, and cinnamon over the butter mixture. Stir to blend. Add the apple pieces and mix.

FENNEL

Fennel is a spice beloved by Italian cooks. Just by themselves, the bulbs can be eaten raw or cooked, and are especially tasty when served with a soothing cheese sauce. Fennel leaves, which have a pleasant licorice taste, can be chopped and added to a variety of soups and sauces, most commonly to fish stews. Fennel seeds are excellent for subtly flavoring everything from Christmas cookies to summer sausage. The ancient Greeks believed that fennel, which grows wild in abundance in almost all parts of the world, gives human beings wisdom, moral courage, and a long and prosperous life.

8. Spread the batter into the prepared pan and bake for 30 minutes, until a skewer inserted in the center comes out clean and dry. Let it cool for 10 to 15 minutes in the pan, then cut into bars. Serve warm or at room temperature.

NOTE: *Make extra fennel sugar, if you like, and store it in a covered jar to marinate and age. It can keep for weeks, like vanilla sugar, and adds a nice flavor to cookies and other baked goods.*

The Richest Lunch Box Cookies Ever

YIELD: ABOUT 4 DOZEN COOKIES

Gourmet cookies have become a staple of the eighties. Start making these for friends and neighbors, and you may find yourself becoming the new Mrs. Fields or David. These lunch box gems make wonderful gifts, too—just fill a tin for birthdays, Christmas gifts, or last-day-on-the-job parties.

2 (3½-ounce) bars caramel-filled Swiss chocolate, such as Lindt
2 ounces bittersweet or semisweet chocolate
2 ounces white chocolate
1 cup pecan halves
1½ cups regular oatmeal (not quick-cooking)
1 cup butter, softened
1½ cups brown sugar, lightly packed
½ teaspoon salt
2 teaspoons vanilla
2 eggs
1½ cups flour
½ teaspoon baking powder
½ teaspoon baking soda

1. Preheat the oven to 350° F.

2. Break the caramel bars into natural sections. Cut the sections into small chunks with a sharp knife. (You may chill the bars first if you like—it helps to keep the caramel from oozing out too much as you cut them.) Set the chunks aside.

SPRING WORK LUNCHES

Get away from the day by heading to the park, riverside, or just to a bench in the sun. Grab some street food on the way, if you like, but bringing your own lunch not only saves precious outdoor time otherwise spent in line at the deli, but usually tastes better too. If you have a refrigerator at work, pack a yogurt sundae: spoon plain or lemon yogurt into a refrigerator container, top it with chopped unpeeled Granny Smith apple (toss it in a little lemon juice first, so it won't darken, and to add a tart touch), golden raisins, dried banana chips, and a drizzle of wild clover honey. It's a lunch filled with vitamins, but you'll feel as if you just snuck out for a sundae in the country.

3. Grate the bittersweet or semisweet chocolate and the white chocolate.

4. Chop the pecans.

5. Place ½ cup of the oatmeal in a blender and blend at high speed until the oatmeal turns to powder.

6. In a large bowl, beat the butter with the sugar, salt, and vanilla until creamy. Add the eggs and beat well. Stir in the flour, powdered oatmeal, remaining oatmeal, baking powder, and baking soda. Add the caramel chunks, both grated chocolates, and the pecans and mix just to combine.

7. Using two spoons or your hands, form balls the size of large walnuts. Place them in rows about 3 inches apart on ungreased cookie sheets. Bake for 10 to 15 minutes until golden brown. Remove the cookies from the sheet and cool on a rack. When cool, store the cookies in an airtight container.

DINNER
in a
FLASH

When busy working people describe how they eat, a complaint that surfaces again and again is that they seldom have enough time or energy at the end of the day to prepare a delicious dinner, let alone one that is as creative as it is nourishing. The good cook on a tight schedule does face a challenge—but certainly not one that is insurmountable. The fact is, some of the most imaginative and satisfying meals can be assembled in thirty minutes or less.

Great everyday, weekday dinners that can be put together in thirty minutes are the focus of this chapter, but keep in mind that these innovative recipes are also superb for all the other times when a cook's schedule is a bit overcrowded—like when a tennis date turns into an unexpected dinner, last minute guests pop into town during the middle of the week, or weekend activities develop into unplanned entertaining.

Sautéed Scallops with Tequila and Lime

YIELD: 2 TO 4 SERVINGS

*T*hese scallops are spiced up in a new way with tequila and red pepper flakes. Those who like a *really* fiery dish can add more red pepper. The flavor of scallops is so delicate, however, that it is easy to overpower—so pepper accordingly. This is a nice fresh dish, easy and quick to prepare on a summer weeknight or any other time.

1 pound sea scallops
1 medium clove garlic
2 scallions
1 tablespoon chopped fresh coriander
½ teaspoon red pepper flakes
1 lime
2 tablespoons tequila
2 tablespoons olive oil

1. Remove the tough connective tissue on the side of the scallops. Slice the scallops into ¼-inch-thick rounds and set aside.

2. Mince the garlic. Slice the scallions on the bias. Combine the garlic, scallions, coriander, and red pepper in a small bowl.

3. Squeeze the juice from the lime into a separate small bowl. Add the tequila and mix together.

4. Heat the olive oil in a large skillet over high heat. Sauté the scallops, tossing continuously, for 1 minute. Reduce the heat slightly and add the garlic-scallion mixture. Cook 2 minutes more. Add the tequila and lime juice, bring the mixture to a boil, then remove the skillet from the heat. Serve immediately.

Lemon Chicken

YIELD: 2 TO 4 SERVINGS

Y ou can have this delicate, very lemony dish on the table in fifteen minutes.

4 tablespoons butter
1 tablespoon grated lemon rind
2 tablespoons unseasoned bread crumbs
1 lemon
2 whole boneless chicken breasts
Salt and freshly ground pepper to taste
4 tablespoons fresh lemon juice
2 tablespoons dry vermouth
1/2 cup heavy cream

1. Preheat the oven to 350° F.

2. Melt 2 tablespoons of the butter in a small saucepan over moderate heat. Remove from the heat and add half the grated lemon rind and all the bread crumbs.

3. Cut the lemon into 1/8-inch slices. Remove the seeds with the point of a knife. Set the slices aside.

4. Cut each whole chicken breast in half. Trim any fat from the breasts and remove the tough white tendon running through the tenderloin on the underside. Using a mallet or heavy spoon, flatten the chicken halves to an even thickness, as thin as possible.

5. Melt the remaining 2 tablespoons of butter in a large skillet over medium-high heat. Sauté the chicken in the melted butter, turning once, for 5 minutes, or until golden. Place the chicken in a shallow baking dish and sprinkle to taste with salt and pepper.

6. Add the lemon juice and remaining grated lemon rind to the hot pan, scraping to deglaze. Add the vermouth and cream and mix until smooth. Taste and correct seasoning. Remove from the heat.

7. Place the lemon slices on top of the chicken. Pour the sauce over the chicken and lemon slices and sprinkle the reserved bread crumb mixture over all.

8. Bake for 10 to 12 minutes, uncovered, until the bread crumbs are slightly browned and the sauce is bubbling. Serve immediately.

TASTY MISCONCEPTIONS

According to the Tufts University Diet and Nutrition Letter, it's *not* true that honey is better for you than sugar, fish is brain food, eating carrots improves eyesight, garlic lowers blood pressure, brown eggs are superior to white, white bread is inferior to whole wheat, an apple a day keeps the doctor away, margarine has fewer calories than butter, fresh vegetables are better than frozen, chocolate aggravates acne, or vitamin E increases virility.

Baked Chicken Breasts with Nectarine

YIELD: 4 SERVINGS

A very simple and very elegant dish that's light in calories and offers a tantalizing marriage of flavors. The delicate blush of the nectarine makes it lovely to serve.

1 large onion
4 medium cloves garlic
2 tablespoons butter
4 boneless half chicken breasts
1 large nectarine
½ cup chicken stock
Salt and freshly ground pepper to taste

1. Preheat the oven to 400° F.

2. Cut the onion into ⅓-inch slices.

3. Mince the garlic cloves.

4. Melt the butter in a medium sauté pan over medium-high heat. Add the sliced onion and sauté until translucent (3 to 5 minutes). Add the garlic and cook, stirring often, 1 to 2 minutes more.

5. Arrange the onions and garlic in an 8 × 8-inch or 7 × 11-inch baking dish.

6. Place the chicken breasts on top of the onion-garlic layer.

7. Halve, pit, and slice the nectarine. Arrange the slices on top of the chicken breasts.

8. Pour the stock over all and sprinkle with salt and pepper. Cover the dish with foil and bake for 15 to 20 minutes.

9. Serve directly from the baking dish with the onions and juices.

The Bildner Burger

YIELD: 4 TO 6 SERVINGS

*A*t our stores, we make these quick dinner burgers thick and juicy, and shaped in an oblong style that makes them perfect to place between the halves of a sliced mini-baguette. The result is, we sell Bildner burgers by the truckload. To bring out the subtle Italian flavors, try garnishing the burgers with chopped tomato and fresh basil tossed in a little olive oil, or topped with a marinated sun-dried tomato and some sliced mozzarella cheese.

4 medium cloves garlic
4 large scallions, green parts only
1 small onion
2 pounds extra lean ground beef
2 tablespoons Worcestershire sauce
¼ cup chopped fresh Italian parsley
¼ cup chopped fresh basil (or 1 tablespoon dried)
2 tablespoons chopped fresh oregano (or 2 teaspoons dried)
1 to 2 tablespoons olive oil
Salt and freshly ground pepper to taste

1. Mince the garlic cloves.

2. Chop the green part of the scallions finely.

3. Chop the onion into ¼-inch dice.

4. Place the ground beef in a large bowl. Add the garlic, scallions, onion, Worcestershire sauce, parsley, basil, and oregano. Mix with your hands just to combine. Shape the meat mixture into 6 thick burgers.

5. Heat the olive oil in a large heavy skillet, over medium-high heat. Cook the burgers, turning once. Sprinkle with salt and pepper and serve.

STUFFED BURGERS

For a quick, fun meal, just form two large, thin patties and stuff them with your favorite fillings. Leave some room around the edges so the stuffing doesn't leak out, then press the edges together and grill or broil. The stuffed burger will cook quickly, so you might wish to preheat a filling like chili. Try these fillings:

♦ Chili and chopped Bermuda onions

♦ Mushrooms sautéed in cream sherry with Parmesan and sour cream

♦ Chopped avocado with salsa and grated Cheddar or Monterey Jack cheese

♦ Red Filling for Tartlettes

♦ Cooked bacon, shredded lettuce, and tomato

♦ Mozzarella with parsley and sun-dried tomatoes

♦ Crumbled feta cheese, chopped Bermuda onion, and a dollop of Thousand Island dressing

♦ Sautéed yellow onion and sliced green peppers, and a sprinkle of toasted sesame seeds

Flank Steak with
Sesame-Cilantro Marinade

YIELD: 6 TO 8 SERVINGS

*T*his simple dish was the hit of a dinner party a friend of ours gave recently. The secret is not in the meat, but in the marinade, which can be made ahead and used with similar results on chicken or tuna steaks. If you can't find fresh cilantro, you can substitute a teaspoon of crushed coriander seeds. The flavor will be slightly different, but still very good. Start the meat off marinading early in the day, and you can have dinner ready in a flash.

2 tablespoons sesame seeds
1 bunch scallions
1 cup fresh cilantro leaves (about 1 large bunch), or 1
    teaspoon crushed coriander seeds
2 cloves garlic
¼ cup sesame oil
¼ cup honey
¼ cup soy sauce
1 teaspoon Tabasco sauce
1 (3-pound) flank steak

1. Place the sesame seeds in a dry skillet over medium heat and toast, stirring continuously, until golden. Remove them from the heat and set aside to cool.

2. Trim the scallions and slice them thinly on the bias. Place them in a medium bowl.

3. Chop the cilantro coarsely. Crush the garlic cloves. Add the cilantro and the garlic to the chopped scallions. Toss to combine.

4. Add the toasted sesame seeds, sesame oil, honey, soy sauce, and Tabasco. Mix well. Keep refrigerated until ready to marinate.

5. To marinate, place the flank steak in a flat dish. Pour the marinade over the meat and turn to coat. Cover with plastic wrap and refrigerate 2 to 6 hours, turning every hour if possible.

6. When ready to cook, prepare the coals or light the grill; or if you are cooking this indoors, preheat the broiler.

7. When the coals are hot, drain the marinade from the steak. Grill the steak for 5 to 7 minutes per side. Serve immediately.

Roast Tenderloin with Watercress Butter

YIELD: 4 SERVINGS

*T*his simple, elegant entree is an example of the usefulness of compound butters, which can be made in just minutes and used to dress up anything from tenderloin to tagliatelle. Develop a few favorites, store them in the refrigerator (they keep for weeks), or freeze them, and you're never at a loss for a sauce.

½ medium bunch fresh watercress
1 (2½-pound) piece of tenderloin of beef
1 tablespoon olive oil
4 tablespoons butter, softened
Salt and freshly ground pepper to taste

1. Preheat the oven to 400° F.

2. Discard the stems from the watercress leaves. Chop the leaves.

3. Trim the tenderloin of all fat and connective tissue. Rub it well on all sides with the olive oil and place it on a rack set in a roasting pan. Roast the tenderloin for 20 to 30 minutes, until the internal temperature (measured with a meat thermometer) reaches 130° to 135° F. for rare.

4. Place the butter in a small bowl and beat it until it is creamy. Add the watercress, salt, and pepper and mix well. Set aside at room temperature for flavors to develop while the tenderloin is roasting.

5. Remove the tenderloin to a cutting board and let it rest for 5 minutes. Slice it as thin as possible and arrange the slices on warmed plates or a serving platter. Top each serving with 1 tablespoon of the watercress butter, or spread all of the butter evenly over the sliced tenderloin on the platter. The heat of the beef will melt the butter and it will create its own sauce. Serve immediately.

COMPOUND BUTTERS

When you make one or two compound butters regularly, you can easily be creative and spontaneous in your cooking.

To make a compound butter, just beat the butter until creamy and blend in a flavoring. You can use it immediately or shape it into a log or a molded form and refrigerate or freeze it. When you use a chilled compound butter, it melts down to form its own sauce. You'll no doubt develop some of your own compound butters, but here are a few of ours to help you get started:

- ◆ Lemon and chive butter for halibut steak

- ◆ Basil and fresh crushed garlic butter for veal, pasta

- ◆ Garlic and sage butter for mushrooms, herb toasts

- ◆ Tarragon butter for pheasant, chicken

- ◆ Watercress and sorrel butter for salmon, trout

- ◆ Ginger, toasted sesame seed, and lemon grass butter for chicken or beef

Christmas Enchiladas

YIELD: 2 TO 4 SERVINGS

Red peppers and green chilies are the stars of this Southwestern entree, hence the funny name. It's a meatless dish that can be put together in no time, and it makes a nice alternative to the usual Mexican midweek dish, the taco. If you'd like to make it a little heartier, just spread the tortilla with a layer of refried beans before you add the filling.

4 medium scallions
1 medium tomato
1 small red bell pepper
1 small red onion
1 (3-ounce) can mild green, chopped chilies
½ cup chopped fresh coriander
3 ounces mild Cheddar cheese
3 ounces Monterey Jack cheese
2 medium cloves garlic
2 tablespoons corn oil
2 tablespoons flour
2 tablespoons chili powder
½ teaspoon ground cumin
1 cup chicken stock
8 corn tortillas (canned, fresh, or frozen and thawed)

1. Preheat the oven to 400° F.

2. Trim and slice the scallions. Dice the tomato, pepper, and onion. Drain the chilies. Place the scallions, tomato, pepper, onion, and chilies in a large bowl. Add the coriander and mix to combine. Set aside.

3. Grate both the cheeses. Mix them together in a small bowl and set aside ½ cup.

4. Mince the garlic.

5. Heat 1 tablespoon of the corn oil in a medium skillet over medium-high heat. Sauté the garlic in the hot oil for 30 seconds. Add the flour, chili powder, and cumin and cook for 30 seconds longer. Remove the skillet from the heat and add the chicken stock, whisking continuously until blended. Return the skillet to the heat, reduce the heat to medium-low, and simmer the mixture for 3 to 5 minutes, until thickened. Set aside.

6. Place a separate ungreased skillet over high heat. Brush the tortillas on both sides with the remaining 1 tablespoon of corn oil. Place them in the hot skillet (one or two at a time, depending on the size of the skillet) for about 2 minutes to soften. Remove them to a plate to cool.

7. To assemble, dip a tortilla in the sauce and place it in an ungreased 9 × 13-inch baking pan. Place 2 to 3 tablespoons of the filling in the middle of the tortilla, top it with 1 tablespoon of the grated cheese, and roll the tortilla up around the filling. Place the enchilada seam-side down in the baking dish. Repeat with the remaining tortillas. Pour any remaining filling over the tortillas and sprinkle them with the grated cheese (both the reserved ½ cup and any remaining). Bake them for 10 to 15 minutes, until the sauce is bubbling and the cheese is melted and slightly browned.

Veal Scallops with Garlic and Artichokes

YIELD: 2 SERVINGS

*S*erved with a simple green salad and a hunk of crusty bread, this *very* Italian dish is a quick and easy affair for weeknight dining, but is also special enough to serve to unexpected dinner guests.

2 medium cloves garlic
1 (9-ounce) box frozen deluxe artichokes, thawed
4 medium veal scallops
2 tablespoons butter
¼ cup white wine
¾ cup heavy cream
1 tablespoon chopped fresh tarragon (or 1 teaspoon dried)
Salt and freshly ground pepper to taste

1. Mince the garlic cloves.

2. Cut the thawed artichokes lengthwise into quarters.

3. Pound the veal scallops until they are thin.

4. Melt 1 tablespoon of the butter in a medium skillet over high heat. Quickly brown the veal scallops in the hot butter (about 1 minute per side), then remove them to a plate.

5. Add the remaining 1 tablespoon butter to the skillet. Add the garlic to the melted butter and sauté, stirring, for 30 seconds. Add the artichoke hearts and sauté, stirring, for 1 to 2 minutes.

6. Pour the white wine into the skillet and bring it to a boil. Cook the mixture for 1 minute, then stir in the cream. Bring the liquid just to a boil, then add the tarragon, salt, and pepper. Reduce the heat to medium and continue to cook, stirring occasionally, until the sauce is thick enough to coat the back of a spoon.

7. Return the veal scallops to the pan and turn them to coat both sides in the hot sauce. Serve immediately, with additional sauce spooned over each serving.

Bowtie Noodles and Poppyseed Butter

YIELD: 4 TO 6 SERVINGS

*H*ere's a lovely, unpretentious pasta dish that's simple to prepare and adds a graceful note to any quick meal. Try it with grilled pork chops and Red Rufus Salad (see Index) for a easy early autumn supper.

1½ tablespoons poppyseeds
4 tablespoons butter, softened
½ teaspoon grated nutmeg
1 teaspoon grated lemon rind
1 teaspoon salt
12 ounces bowtie pasta noodles (or rotini, shells, or corkscrew pasta)
Freshly ground pepper to taste

1. Place the poppyseeds in a small ungreased sauté pan over medium heat. Toast, shaking often, for 5 to 10 minutes, to release the full flavor. Let cool for 1 to 2 minutes.

2. Combine the toasted poppyseeds, softened butter, nutmeg, and lemon rind in a small bowl. Set aside.

3. Bring a large pot of water with 1 teaspoon of salt to a boil. Cook the pasta, stirring often, for 10 to 12 minutes, until tender but firm to a bite.

4. Drain the noodles and place them in a serving dish. Add the reserved butter mixture with salt and pepper to taste, and toss to melt the butter and coat the noodles. Serve immediately.

Asparagus with Citrus Butter

YIELD: 6 SERVINGS

*T*he tart citrus butter is easier to make than traditional hollandaise sauce and lower in cholesterol. Try citrus butter on other fresh green vegetables like broccoli, fiddleheads, and Brussels sprouts.

1 bunch fresh young asparagus
¼ cup butter
3 tablespoons lemon juice
3 tablespoons orange juice

1. Trim off any woody ends of the asparagus. Bring 2 to 3 inches of water to a boil in a large pot or steamer. Steam or blanch the asparagus just until it is tender and the color is bright (2 to 3 minutes).

2. Melt the butter in a small saucepan over low heat. Stir in the lemon and orange juices.

3. Pour the citrus butter over the steamed asparagus and serve immediately.

PEPPED-UP VEGGIES

Put these inspired veggies next to grilled chicken or fish for a fast reward at the end of a long working day.

◆ Make a quick, zesty cheese sauce by swirling equal parts ricotta and blue cheese with a little sour cream in the blender. Pour over hot cauliflower or potatoes.

◆ Toss chopped fresh parsley, minced garlic, and a little olive oil with steamed broccoli or asparagus tips.

◆ Try some Compound Butters with a variety of steamed vegteables—tarragon butter with parsnips, for instance, or watercress and sorrel butter on zucchini and summer squash.

◆ Stir-fry broccoli florets with water chestnuts and Chinese cabbage to go with Spicy Peanut Chicken.

◆ Sauté kernels of fresh corn with red peppers and jalapeños.

◆ Toss steamed carrots with sliced apples and curry with a little cream.

◆ Sauté pear wedges with Bermuda onion slices and a little red wine.

Tzatziki Couscous

YIELD: 6 SERVINGS

*T*zatziki is a Greek yogurt-cucumber dip that is usually flavored with mint. We changed the mint to oregano and blended it with couscous to make a quick, delicious side dish that can be served equally well warm or cold. It's superb with lamb or chicken shish kebabs, for a quick week-night meal.

1 cup couscous
1 tablespoon olive oil
1 cup boiling water
1 small clove garlic
1 medium cucumber
¾ cup plain yogurt
2 tablespoons lemon juice
1 tablespoon dried oregano (or ¼ cup chopped fresh)
Salt and freshly ground pepper to taste

1. Place the couscous in a medium bowl. Add the olive oil and toss well to coat. Pour the boiling water over the couscous and stir, then cover and let sit for 5 minutes.

2. While the couscous sits, mince the garlic. Peel and dice the cucumber.

3. In a small bowl, mix together the yogurt, lemon juice, oregano, salt, pepper, garlic, and cucumber.

4. Uncover the couscous. Add the yogurt mixture and toss well to combine. Serve immediately or chill and serve cold.

Perfect Peach Cheesecake

YIELD: 6 TO 8 SERVINGS

*T*here are people who simply refuse to bake—so this rich dessert recipe is perfect for them . . . and for the rest of us. It's quick to make—about thirty minutes—but for the best texture it should be refrigerated overnight before it's served. If you can find Pêcher Mignon (a white peach liqueur), we suggest you try it. If not, any good peach brandy or schnapps will do nicely.

CRUST:
6 tablespoons butter
1 12-ounce box Destrooper Butter Waffle Cookies (or other crisp butter cookie)
2 graham crackers

FILLING:
1/2 cup heavy cream, chilled
1 tablespoon plus 1/3 cup sugar
8 ounces cream cheese, softened
1 cup sour cream
1 teaspoon vanilla
1/4 teaspoon salt
3 tablespoons Pêcher Mignon or other peach brandy
1/3 cup peach conserve, jam, or marmalade

1. To make the crust, melt the butter in a small saucepan over medium-low heat.

2. Place the cookies and the graham crackers in the bowl of a food processor fitted with a steel blade. Process to grind to a fine powder. Add the melted butter and process for a few seconds, just to blend. Press the crumb mixture into the bottom and sides of a 9-inch pie plate.

3. To make the filling, in a medium bowl beat the cream with 1 tablespoon of the sugar until barely stiff. Set aside.

4. Place the cream cheese in the bowl of an electric mixer. Add the remaining 1/3 cup sugar and beat at high speed, until the mixture is soft and fluffy. Remove the bowl from the mixer and, using a spoon, stir in (do not beat) the sour cream, vanilla, salt, and peach liqueur. Using a spatula, fold the whipped cream into the cream cheese mixture. Pour the mixture into the prepared pie shell.

5. Spoon the peach conserve in 4 thin strips across the cheesecake. Carefully marble it by drawing a spoon or knife through the mixture, without stirring up the crust. Cover and refrigerate until set, for several hours or overnight.

Not Just Another Pretty Peanut Butter Pie

YIELD: 6 TO 8 SERVINGS

Located in Boston's historic Faneuil Hall Marketplace, Trombly's Peanut Butter Fantasies, makers of delicious all-natural peanut butter products, tell us that there is a right way and a wrong way to make peanut butter pie. Happily for us, they told us the right way. It's easy, it's fast. For fun or an unusual twist you might try any of Trombly's special flavored peanut butters—Banana Crunch, Honey Cinnamon, Chocolate Raspberry, or Chunky Maple Cashew.

1 cup heavy cream, chilled
4 ounces cream cheese, softened
1 cup confectioners' sugar
1/3 cup creamy peanut butter
1/2 cup milk
1 (9-inch) prepared graham cracker or cookie crust (see note)

NOTE: You may use a purchased piecrust, or prepare your own according to the crust instructions given for Perfect Peach Cheesecake (see Index).

1. In a large bowl, beat the cream just until soft peaks begin to form. Refrigerate.

2. Beat the cream cheese in a medium bowl until soft and fluffy.

3. Add the sugar and peanut butter to the cream cheese and beat until smooth. While beating, slowly add the milk. Continue beating until smooth and well blended.

4. Remove the cream from the refrigerator and whisk lightly to blend. Using a spatula or flat spoon, fold the whipped cream into the peanut butter mixture. Pour the pie filling into the prepared crumb crust and place in the freezer. When the pie is firm (about 4 hours), wrap it tightly in plastic wrap and keep it frozen until ready to serve.

5. When ready to serve, slice the pie into servings while still frozen. Let the slices stand for 5 to 10 minutes to soften. Keep any unused pie (up to 4 days) tightly covered in the freezer.

Almond Genoise

YIELD: 6 SERVINGS

*T*his elegant cake is a terrific traveler, great for picnics or long distance holiday traveling, or for working lunches, and is a wonderful gift item too. But, best of all, the batter can be made in one mixing bowl in 15 minutes or less.

1 cup slivered almonds
½ cup butter plus ½ tablespoon for pan
3 eggs
¾ cup sugar
1 teaspoon almond extract
¼ teaspoon salt
¾ cup all-purpose flour
¼ cup cornstarch
½ teaspoon baking powder
¼ cup Amaretto liqueur
Confectioners' sugar for topping

1. Preheat the oven to 350° F.

2. Spread the almonds in a layer on an ungreased baking sheet and toast them in the oven for 5 to 7 minutes, until browned. Let them cool for a minute, then place them in the bowl of a food processor fitted with a steel blade. Pulse to grind.

3. Melt ½ cup of the butter in a small saucepan over low heat. Set it aside to cool. Butter a 9 × 7-inch pan with the remaining ½ tablespoon of butter.

4. Place the eggs, sugar, almond extract, and salt in a large bowl and beat for about 5 minutes until foamy (almost white) and thick (a wide, heavy ribbon should fall from the beaters when they are lifted from the bowl.)

5. Sift the flour, cornstarch, and baking powder onto the cake batter. And the ground almonds. Fold the dry ingredients into the eggs using a spatula or flat spoon.

6. Pour the melted butter into the batter in a slow stream, folding in with the spatula or spoon until the butter is incorporated.

7. Pour the batter into the buttered pan and bake for 20 to 25 minutes, until golden. Invert and unmold the cake gently onto a rack and let it cool to lukewarm. Place it on a serving platter and punch small holes in the top of the cake with a skewer. Brush the top of the cake with the Amaretto and let it sit to mellow and cool completely, about 30 minutes. Just before serving, dust the top of the cake with sifted confectioners' sugar.

Summer Sabayon

YIELD: 4 SERVINGS

*O*ur version of this classic French dessert has a touch of Chambord and is a little less sweet than most. We've teamed it with summer berries, but it can also be poured over sliced fresh peaches, pears, even seedless grapes. For a nice winter variation, replace the Chambord with a bit of bourbon or a hearty liqueur and serve it over a stewed fruit compote.

4 egg yolks
⅓ cup sugar
1 teaspoon vanilla
¼ cup Chambord liqueur
¼ cup white wine
1 pint each fresh raspberries, blueberries, and strawberries

1. In a heatproof bowl, beat the egg yolks and sugar until very pale and thick. Slowly whisk in the vanilla, liqueur, and wine.

2. Place the bowl over a saucepan of barely simmering water, and continue whisking until the sauce thickens. Do not let the water get hotter than a simmmer.

3. When the sauce is thickened, remove the bowl from the hot water and continue to beat for 2 or 3 minutes. Place the bowl over a pan of ice and continue whisking until the sauce is thoroughly chilled. The sabayon may be served immediately or refrigerated until serving time.

4. When ready to serve, rinse all the berries and hull the strawberries. Mix the berries together in a large bowl and pass the sabayon separately.

MAKE-AHEAD DINNERS

*A*t Bildner's one of the largest categories of daily sales we do is in our chef-prepared take-out foods, especially at the dinner hour. We've learned that people don't want to sacrifice the pleasure of serving a good home-cooked meal just because time is short—but sometimes they need a little bit of help to accomplish that goal.

Our chefs have become experts at making dinners ahead of time, perfect for any planned or unplanned event. The same recipes that are popular with our customers will work just as well for you at home, saving you precious time and energy but not skimping on the reward of a hot home-cooked dinner.

Among other things, we've found that these recipes are great for older kids of working parents who get home at unpredictable hours. Great for the working parents, too.

Bildner's Famous Clam Chowder

YIELD: 4 TO 6 SERVINGS

*L*ike most chowders, this one is best if allowed to sit overnight. That gives the distinctive flavors a chance to develop and blend together. The smoked clams in this recipe enhance the smoky hint of bacon and make this chowder more flavorful than many.

4 (¼-inch) thick slices slab bacon (3½ to 4 ounces total)
1 large onion
1 large potato
Salt and freshly ground pepper to taste
1 tablespoon flour
1 cup clam juice, fresh or bottled
3 cups milk
1 cup heavy cream
1 pint fresh shucked clams with juice (not canned)
1 3-ounce can smoked clams, drained
¼ cup chopped fresh Italian parsley

1. Cut the bacon crosswise into ¼-inch pieces. Place it in a large kettle over medium heat. Cook, stirring occasionally, until crisp. Remove the bacon with a slotted spoon and place it on paper towels to drain.

2. Dice the onion and potato. Add the onion to the hot bacon fat and cook for about 3 minutes, stirring, until it is translucent. Add the potato and brown lightly. Season with salt and pepper to taste. Sprinkle the potato and onion with the flour and cook, stirring, for 2 minutes.

3. Stirring quickly, add the clam juice, milk, and cream. Bring the mixture to a boil, continuing to stir. Lower the heat and simmer the chowder, covered, for 20 minutes.

4. After 20 minutes, add the fresh clams and their juice, the smoked clams, and the reserved bacon pieces. Cook the chowder for 2 minutes more. (If making ahead, refrigerate at this point.) Top with chopped parsley and serve.

Bildner's Chili

YIELD: 8 TO 10 SERVINGS

Good chili, like chowder, gets better after a couple of days. We sell so much of this chili in our Boston stores it's a wonder Boston isn't famous for chili instead of baked beans. If you prefer, you can make this classic chili with strips of lean beef rather than ground beef. Try it with the Southwest Salad Bowl and Spicy Corn Bread (see Index for recipes) for a Tex-Mex meal.

3 medium onions
10 medium cloves garlic
2 tablespoons vegetable oil
4 pounds lean ground beef
1 tablespoon sugar
6 tablespoons chili powder
1 teaspoon cayenne pepper
1 tablespoon ground cumin
1 teaspoon dried oregano
Salt and freshly ground pepper to taste
2 tablespoons corn flour (masa harina—in the imported foods section)
3 (3-ounce) cans chopped mild green chilies, drained (or hot if you prefer your chili very spicy)
2 (16-ounce) cans red kidney beans, drained
1 (1-pound, 13-ounce) can whole tomatoes, undrained
1 (6-ounce) can tomato paste
1 cup beef broth
Grated Cheddar or Monterey Jack cheese, diced red onion, sour cream, and chopped green chilies for topping

1. Chop the onions into ½-inch dice. Mince the garlic.

2. Heat the oil in a large, heavy non-aluminum pot over medium-high heat until hot but not smoking. Sauté the chopped onions and garlic, for about 3 minutes, stirring, until the onions are translucent. Add the ground beef and sear, breaking up any large chunks of beef with a spoon.

3. In a small bowl, mix together the sugar, chili powder, cayenne, cumin, oregano, salt, pepper, and corn flour. Sprinkle the mixture over the meat, reduce the heat to medium, and stir. Add the chopped chilies, kidney beans, canned tomatoes with their liquid, tomato paste, and beef

---

TEN THINGS THAT HAPPILY GET BETTER WITH, TIME

- Red wine
- Split-pea soup
- Cher
- Camembert cheese
- The White Album
- Bildner's Chili
- Jack Nicklaus
- Irish whiskey cake
- Blue jeans
- Newlyweds' cooking

broth. Stir well, breaking up the tomatoes with the spoon. Bring the chili to a boil, raising the heat if necessary.

4. Reduce the heat to low and simmer the chili for 2 to 3 hours. Serve with grated cheese, diced red onion, sour cream, and chopped green chilies to top.

Texas-Style BBQ Brisket of Beef

YIELD: 6 TO 8 SERVINGS

*H*ere is a delicious make-ahead dish that can be frozen or simply kept for a few days in the fridge for a quick week-night supper. Many barbecue recipes are either overloaded with sweetness or too hot to handle. This tangy variation is bound to please everyone. Serve it over noodles or with crusty bread.

1 teaspoon ground cumin
1 teaspoon dried coriander
1 (4-pound) beef brisket
2 tablespoons vegetable oil
1 medium onion
1 medium carrot
1 medium stalk celery
3 large cloves garlic
½ teaspoon hot red pepper flakes
2 tablespoons brown sugar
½ cup molasses
½ cup red wine vinegar
1 (1-pound, 13-ounce) can tomato sauce

1. In a small bowl, mix the cumin and coriander together.

2. Trim the beef brisket of all fat. Rub the cumin and coriander into all sides of the meat.

3. Heat the oil in a large saucepan or Dutch oven, over medium-high heat. Brown the brisket in the hot oil, searing all sides well.

4. While the brisket is browning, dice the onion and carrot. Dice the celery and mince the garlic.

5. When the brisket is well seared, remove it from the pan. Add the onion, carrot, celery, and garlic to the oil and sauté to brown lightly. Add the pepper flakes and continue to sauté for 2 minutes.

6. Stir in the brown sugar and molasses and cook for 1 minute. Add the vinegar and tomato sauce and stir to combine.

7. Return the brisket to the pot. Bring the liquid to a boil, then lower the heat and simmer, covered, until the brisket is tender, about 3 hours. A knife should glide in and out of the meat easily. Serve sliced, with some sauce spooned over each serving.

Veal Goulash with Garlic and Caraway

YIELD: 6 TO 8 SERVINGS

*T*his outstanding goulash can be made ahead of time and frozen for up to two months without losing a whit of flavor or texture. It's also been a favorite weekend dish—and video food—of a Bildner store manager who insists that the best way to serve it is over noodles, with a good bread and a crispy stir-fry side dish, something like Jerusalem artichokes and carrots.

3 large cloves garlic
1 teaspoon caraway seeds
1 teaspoon dried marjoram
3 pounds boneless veal (shoulder or stew meat)
4 tablespoons vegetable or olive oil
1 large onion
2 teaspoons sweet paprika
1 teaspoon hot paprika
2 tablespoons tomato paste
1 (16-ounce) can Italian tomatoes (with liquid)
Salt and freshly ground pepper to taste

1. Mince the garlic. Place it in a small bowl and mix in the caraway and marjoram.

PAPRIKA

Say "paprika" to some cooks, and they'll think of the dreaded orange dusting on the creamed chicken in their school cafeteria lunch line. A flavorless, rather ineffective, attempt at a garnish.

That's not paprika, that's poor presentation. First, paprika isn't orange, but a deep, rich red. Paprika is a spice made from a sweet variety of red pepper—some are hot, some are mild. All have a sweet aroma, but Hungarian paprika is known for having the fullest, spiciest flavor.

Second, it's not—or shouldn't be—flavorless. Paprika gets its reputation for dullness because it doesn't have a long shelf life. Buy it in small quantities and use it in dishes like veal goulash or sautéed chicken instead of as a garnish, and you'll never liken it to brick dust again.

2. Cut the veal into 1- to 2-inch cubes. Add half the garlic mixture to the meat.

3. Heat 2 tablespoons of the oil in a Dutch oven. Brown the veal cubes in the hot oil in two batches, stirring occasionally to brown on all sides. Remove the browned veal to a plate.

4. While the veal browns, chop the onion.

5. When all the veal has been browned and removed from the pan, add the chopped onion to the hot oil remaining in the pan and sauté, stirring, for 3 to 4 minutes, until translucent. Add both the paprikas, stir, and cook for 1 minute. Add the tomato paste, tomatoes, salt, and pepper. Stir, scraping to deglaze the pan, and crush the tomatoes with the back of the spoon.

6. Return all the veal to the pan, bring the liquid to a boil, then lower the heat to a simmer and cover the pan. Simmer the goulash for 2 hours, or until a skewer slides easily in and out of the meat.

7. Just before serving (or before refrigerating, if making ahead), stir in the remaining half of the garlic mixture.

Spicy Peanut Chicken

YIELD: 4 SERVINGS

We've found this to be a nearly perfect summer dinner dish to eat cold when you get home from work tired and hungry. Since it keeps so well, it's also a good picnic food. We like to make it with drumsticks, but it works equally well with breasts, thighs, or wings.

2 cloves garlic
5 tablespoons soy sauce
3 tablespoons water
1 tablespoon lemon juice
1 tablespoon brown sugar
1 teaspoon red pepper flakes
½ teaspoon ground cinnamon
6 tablespoons creamy peanut butter
4 tablespoons butter
4 large chicken legs (about 3 to 3½ pounds)
1 cup unsalted peanuts

1. Chop the garlic coarsely.

2. In a blender, combine the chopped garlic with the soy sauce, water, lemon juice, brown sugar, red pepper flakes, and cinnamon. Blend to combine. Add the peanut butter and blend until smooth.

3. Melt the butter in a small saucepan over medium-high heat. Add the melted butter to the peanut butter mixture and blend until smooth.

4. Place the chicken legs in a non-aluminum pan and pour the marinade over them. Marinate in the refrigerator for 12 hours or overnight.

5. Preheat the oven to 375° F.

6. Chop the peanuts finely.

7. Roll one side of the chicken legs in the chopped peanuts. Place, peanut-side up, on an ungreased baking sheet. Bake for 30 to 35 minutes. Remove from the oven, let cool slightly, then refrigerate until needed. Serve chilled or at room temperature.

Chicken Pot Pie

YIELD: 6 TO 8 SERVINGS

*H*ere's a classic make-ahead meal that freezes beautifully. We make it with a mixture of white and dark meat, but you can use just white if you prefer. At Bildner's, these pies are a favorite with single diners and families alike.

FILLING:
1¼ pounds boneless chicken breast (2 whole)
2 chicken legs (about 1½ pounds)
¾ pound carrots
1 medium onion
5 tablespoons butter
5 tablespoons flour
4 cups chicken stock
1 cup small frozen peas, thawed
Salt and freshly ground pepper to taste

CRUST:
2 cups flour
1 tablespoon baking powder
½ teaspoon salt
¼ cup butter, chilled
¾ cup milk

1. To make the filling, fill a large saucepan with water and bring it to the boil. Reduce the heat to a simmer and poach the chicken breasts and legs. Remove the chicken breasts after 12 minutes and let them cool. Continue to poach the legs for another 13 minutes, for a total of 25 minutes. Remove the legs from the water and let them cool. Raise the heat to boiling.

2. Cut the carrots into ½-inch pieces. Blanch the carrot pieces in the boiling water until tender, about 10 to 15 minutes. Drain them and set aside.

3. Dice the onion. In a medium-size heavy saucepan, melt the butter over medium heat. Cook the onion for 3 to 4 minutes, stirring often, until translucent.

4. Add the flour, whisking until smooth. Cook for 5 minutes, stirring often. Do not let the flour brown—reduce the heat if necessary.

5. Slowly whisk the stock into the flour mixture. Bring the liquid to a boil, whisking to keep the sauce smooth. Lower the heat and simmer for 25 minutes.

6. While the sauce is simmering, skin and bone the chicken legs, and cut the meat into large chunks. Trim the breasts and cut them into large chunks.

7. In an ungreased 2-quart baking dish, combine the chicken, carrots, and peas. Sprinkle with salt and pepper. Season the sauce with additional salt and pepper to taste and pour over the chicken and vegetables.

8. Preheat the oven to 350° F.

9. To make the crust, combine the flour, baking powder, and salt in a medium bowl. Using a pastry blender or two knives, cut the chilled butter into the flour mixture until the mixture is of uniform texture.

10. Add the milk, tossing and pressing the mixture together with a fork to combine. Place the dough on the counter and knead it for 20 strokes. Roll the dough out on a floured counter or board until it is large enough to overlap each edge of the baking dish by about ½ inch, and about ⅓ inch thick. Place the crust over the chicken mixture. (Try not to stretch or pull the crust as you work, or it will shrink as it bakes.) Crimp the edges with your fingers or a fork and cut or poke steam vents in the crust.

11. Place the baking dish on a baking sheet and bake the pie for 30 to 45 minutes, until the crust is golden brown.

Red Cabbage Harvest Rolls

YIELD: 6 SERVINGS

*T*hese unusual rolls require some extra time for assembly, but they reheat well and keep for days. This alternative to traditional stuffed cabbage is flavored with a harvest bounty of pork, apples, brown and wild rice, carrots, walnuts, and cider.

⅓ cup brown rice
⅓ cup wild rice
1 large head red cabbage
½ cup shelled walnuts
2 medium carrots
1 medium onion
1 large tart apple, such as Granny Smith
1 lemon
½ pound ground pork
1 egg
1 teaspoon grated orange rind
Salt and freshly ground pepper to taste
2 tablespoons lemon juice
1½ cups chicken broth
½ cup apple cider
1 tablespoon flour
¼ cup heavy cream

1. Cook both rices separately, according to individual package directions.

2. While the rices cook, preheat the oven to 350° F.

3. Fill a large pot with water and bring it to a boil over high heat. Cut a 2-inch slice off the core end of the cabbage. Using a paring knife, cut a large cone into the core-end, removing as much of the core as possible. Place the cabbage in the boiling water. Let it boil for 2 to 3 minutes. Remove the cabbage from the water. Using tongs, take off the 2 outer leaves of the cabbage and put them in a large bowl. Return the cabbage to the boiling water for a few minutes, then remove the next 2 outer leaves. Continue doing this until you have removed 12 leaves, then boil the remaining cabbage for 10 more minutes. Remove the cooked cabbage to a plate to cool, separate from the 12 leaves.

4. While the cabbage and rices are cooking, prepare the filling. Spread the walnuts in a layer on an ungreased baking sheet and toast them in the oven for 7 minutes until browned. Let them cool, then chop them coarsely.

5. Keep the oven temperature at 350° F.

6. Shred the carrots. Dice the onion and apple. Place the nuts, carrots, onion, and apple in a medium bowl.

7. Cut the lemon into 12 thin slices. Remove the seeds with the point of a knife.

8. When the rices are cooked, add them to the bowl with the nuts and chopped vegetables. Add the ground pork, egg, orange rind, salt, pepper, and lemon juice. Mix everything together well.

9. Chop the cooked inside of the cabbage. Add 1 cup of the chopped cabbage to the pork mixture and mix well. Spread the remaining chopped cabbage in a large (9 × 13-inch ungreased baking dish.

10. Devein the 12 reserved leaves by slicing off the raised vein so that it is flush with the rest of the leaf. Place 1 leaf, deveined side down, on a flat surface. Place ⅓ cup of the filling in the middle of the leaf and roll it up, folding in the sides of the leaf to enclose the filling completely. Place the cabbage roll over the chopped cabbage in the baking dish, seam-side down. Repeat with the remaining leaves.

11. Pour the chicken broth and cider over the cabbage rolls and top each with a lemon slice.

12. Cover the dish tightly with foil (it may be made ahead and refrigerated at this point, or cooked, then refrigerated and reheated later) and place it in the oven to bake for 1½ hours, until the cabbage leaves are tender.

13. Remove the cabbage rolls and the chopped cabbage with a slotted spoon and arrange them on a serving platter. Pour the juices into a medium saucepan and place it over high heat. Whisk the flour into the juices and bring the liquid to a boil. Add the cream, reduce the heat to medium, and cook the sauce for 2 to 3 minutes. Pour it over the cabbage rolls and serve.

Cross-Country Baked Potatoes

YIELD: 2 SERVINGS

*T*hese four recipes are designed for two people, but can easily be doubled. If you have a microwave at work, they make quick delicious lunches to reheat. And they are perfect to bake ahead, stuff, and then reheat just before dinner, too. You can cut down on the baking time by doing the initial baking in a microwave. Great for easy after-work meals, or relaxed weekend living. Serve with a green salad.

New England Stuffed Potatoes

2 large Maine potatoes
1 slice cob-smoked ham (about 2 ounces) (see note)
½ Golden Delicious apple
¼ cup plus 2 tablespoons grated Colby cheese
2 tablespoons milk
1 tablespoon butter
½ teaspoon salt
Freshly ground pepper to taste

NOTE: Cob-smoked ham is cured by smoking with a fire of dried corncobs. It is found in New England and can be ordered by mail through many smokehouses.

1. Preheat the oven to 400° F.

2. Bake the potatoes for 45 to 60 minutes, or until soft when pierced with a skewer.

3. While the potatoes bake, dice the ham slice and quarter, peel, and core the apple.

4. Place the diced ham and apple in a small bowl, add ¼ cup of the grated cheese, and mix.

5. When the potatoes are done, remove them from the oven.

6. Lower the oven temperature to 350° F.

7. Slit each potato lengthwise or cut away a small oval to make a "canoe." Using a small spoon, scoop out the interior of the potatoes, leaving a ¼- to ½-inch-thick shell. Place the potato pulp in a medium bowl and mash with the milk, butter, salt, and pepper. Stir in the ham mixture.

8. Pile the filling back into the potato shells, mounding the mixture over the top. Place the stuffed potatoes on a foil-lined cookie sheet, or cake pan. On each potato, sprinkle the top of the stuffing with 1 tablespoon of the grated cheese and bake for 15 to 25 minutes, until the cheese is melted and the potatoes are heated through.

Midwestern Stuffed Potatoes

2 large Idaho potatoes
1 teaspoon plus 1 tablespoon butter
1 (4-ounce) tenderloin steak
1 scallion, green part only
¼ cup plus 2 teaspoons sour cream
Salt and freshly ground pepper to taste

1. Preheat the oven to 400° F.

2. Bake the potatoes for 45 to 60 minutes, or until soft when pierced with a skewer.

3. While the potatoes bake, melt 1 teaspoon of the butter in a small skillet over medium-high heat. Panfry the tenderloin in the melted butter for 2 to 3 minutes per side. (The steak should be medium-rare, at most.) Remove the skillet from the heat and set aside to cool. When cool, cut the tenderloin in thin strips.

4. Slice the scallion thinly on the bias. Set aside.

5. When the potatoes are done, remove them from the oven.

6. Lower the oven temperature to 350° F.

7. Slit each potato open lengthwise or cut away a small oval to make a "canoe." Using a small spoon, scoop out the interior of the potatoes, leaving a ¼- to ½-inch-thick shell. Place the potato pulp in a medium bowl and mash with 1 tablespoon butter, ¼ cup of the sour cream, salt, and pepper. Stir in the tenderloin strips.

8. Pile the filling into the potato shells, mounding the mixture over the top. On each potato, spread the top of the stuffing with 1 teaspoon of the sour cream. Sprinkle the scallion slices over the sour cream.

9. Place the potatoes on a foil-lined cookie sheet or cake pan and bake for 15 to 25 minutes, until heated through.

Southwestern Stuffed Potatoes

2 large Idaho potatoes
½ small red onion (about 2 ounces)
½ tablespoon vegetable oil
½ tablespoon canned mild or hot green chilies
½ cup rinsed and drained canned pinto beans
¼ cup sour cream
¼ cup plus 2 tablespoons grated Monterey Jack cheese
1 large pinch of ground cumin (optional)
½ teaspoon salt
Freshly ground pepper to taste

1. Preheat the oven to 400° F.

2. Bake the potatoes for 45 to 60 minutes, or until soft when pierced with a skewer.

3. While the potatoes bake, dice the onion. Heat the oil in a small skillet over high heat. Add the onion and sauté for 3 minutes, until translucent. Chop the chilies and add them to the onion. Continue cooking for another minute. Add the pinto beans and heat through.

4. When the potatoes are done, remove them from the oven.

5. Lower the oven temperature to 350° F.

6. Slit each potato open lengthwise or cut away a small oval to make a "canoe." Using a small spoon, scoop out the interior of the potatoes, leaving a ¼- to ½-inch-thick shell. Place the potato pulp in a medium bowl and mash with the sour cream. Add the bean mixture, ¼ cup of the grated cheese, cumin, salt, and pepper. Stir to combine.

7. Pile the filling into the shells and mound the mixture up over the top.

8. Place the potatoes on a foil-lined cookie sheet or cake pan. On each potato, sprinkle the top of the stuffing with 1 tablespoon of the grated cheese. Bake for 15 to 25 minutes, or until cheese is melted and the stuffing is heated through.

Southern Stuffed Potatoes

2 large sweet potatoes
1 large Vidalia onion (about 8 ounces) (see note)
2 tablespoons butter
2 tablespoons chopped fresh parsley
3 tablespoons heavy cream
½ teaspoon freshly grated nutmeg
½ teaspoon salt
Freshly ground pepper to taste

NOTE: *A sweet variety of onion, grown exclusively in Vidalia, Georgia.*

1. Preheat the oven to 400° F.

2. Bake the sweet potatoes for 45 to 60 minutes, or until soft when pierced with a skewer.

3. While the potatoes bake, cut the onion into ¼-inch slices. Melt 1 tablespoon of the butter in a small skillet over medium-high heat. Add the onion slices and sauté until soft, about 5 to 10 minutes. Add the chopped parsley, remove from the heat, and set aside.

4. When the potatoes are done, remove them from the oven.

5. Lower the oven temperature to 350° F.

6. Slit each potato open lengthwise or cut away a small oval to make a "canoe." Using a small spoon, scoop out the interior of the potatoes, leaving a ¼- to ½-inch-thick shell. Place the potato pulp in a medium bowl and mash with remaining 1 tablespoon of the butter, 2 tablespoons of the heavy cream, nutmeg, salt, and pepper. Stir in the onion mixture.

7. Pile the filling into the potato shells, mounding the mixture over the top.

8. Place the potatoes on a foil-lined cookie sheet or cake pan. Over the top of each potato, pour ½ tablespoon of heavy cream. Bake until heated through, 15 to 25 minutes.

Pasta Salad with Shrimp and Pine Nuts

YIELD: 4 TO 6 SERVINGS AS A MAIN DISH;
6 TO 8 SERVINGS AS AN ACCOMPANIMENT

One of our distinctive pasta suppliers, Al Dente, sent this interesting and versatile recipe along. It's a splendid make-ahead meal, just right for the simplest of late night suppers, or delicious as a side dish at cookouts and picnics.

DRESSING:
½ *cup olive oil*
¼ *cup lemon juice*
1 *tablespoon Dijon-style mustard*
½ *cup chopped fresh Italian parsley*
Salt and freshly ground pepper to taste

SALAD:
1 *pound medium raw, unpeeled fresh shrimp*
⅓ *cup pine nuts (approximately 1 [2-ounce] jar)*
2 *medium red bell peppers*
2 *medium zucchini*
4 *scallions*
12 *ounces fresh fettucine*

1. Combine all the dressing ingredients in a blender and blend until smooth. Set aside at room temperature.

2. Bring a large pot of water to a boil over high heat. Place the shrimp in the boiling water, reduce the heat to medium, and return the water to the boil. Poach the shrimp in the simmering water for 3 to 5 minutes, just until they turn pink. Remove the shrimp from the water and cool. When cool enough to handle, shell and devein the shrimp and place them in a large bowl.

3. Place the pine nuts in a dry medium sauté pan over low heat. Toast the nuts until golden, 5 to 10 minutes, stirring often. Set them aside to cool.

4. Dice the peppers and zucchini. Cut the scallions on the bias into ¼-inch slices. Add all the vegetables, along with the cooled pine nuts, to the shrimp.

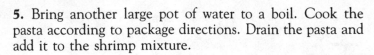

5. Bring another large pot of water to a boil. Cook the pasta according to package directions. Drain the pasta and add it to the shrimp mixture.

6. Pour the dressing over the mixture and toss well to coat the pasta, shrimp, and vegetables.

7. Serve at once at room temperature; or chill, then bring the salad to room temperature before serving.

Hazelnut Pesto Sauce

YIELD: ABOUT 4 CUPS

*T*his rich, nutty-tasting, easy-to-make sauce keeps extremely well. Toss it with fusilli, or spread it over grilled chicken or veal chops. Versatility is the name of the game here. Just be sure to toast the hazelnuts thoroughly to bring out their full-bodied flavor.

1 cup shelled hazelnuts
3 cups fresh basil leaves
3 medium cloves garlic
1½ cups grated Parmesan cheese
¾ cup extra virgin olive oil
¼ cup hazelnut oil
Salt and freshly ground pepper to taste

1. Preheat the oven to 350° F.

2. Spread the hazelnuts on an ungreased jelly roll pan or other large flat pan with sides. Toast the nuts for 10 to 15 minutes. When the nuts are ready, the skins will crack and the nuts will be fragrant. Remove the pan from the oven and pour the nuts into a clean tea towel while they are still hot. Wrap the towel around the nuts and rub to remove the skins.

3. Wash the basil well. Pat it dry or spin it in a salad spinner.

4. Mince the garlic.

5. Place the hazelnuts in the bowl of a food processor fitted with a steel blade. Process for about 30 seconds, turning the machine off every 10 seconds or so to check the texture. (They should be well ground, but not powdered.) Remove the ground nuts to a small bowl.

6. Place the basil and garlic in the food processor (there is no need to clean it between grinding the hazelnuts and processing the rest) and process just enough to chop the basil. Add the cheese and process to blend. With the machine running, add the olive oil and hazelnut oil in a steady, slow stream. Continue to process just to blend.

7. Add the ground nuts, salt, and pepper, and process just to blend. Use immediately, store in the refrigerator up to 2 weeks, or freeze up to 4 months. If storing, stir to recombine any separated ingredients before using.

J. Bildner & sons

Special Occasions

Many years ago, Joe Bildner, the family's first grocer, had a habit of inviting his customers home to dinner on an impromptu basis. To Mr. Joe, every meal was a special occasion. Today at Bildner's, our customers rely on us for great food and good advice about special occasions of all kinds, such as an impending family gathering, an elegant dinner party for eight, an anniversary supper, or just a simple meal to woo that reluctant someone.

Pulling out the stops for a special occasion meal requires some extra work and solid planning. You'll find you have to invest more time preparing the distinctive recipes found in these festive concluding chapters than those found in other sections of the book, but we're certain you'll find it to be labor well spent. If you're like Mr. Joe, you'll probably find yourself thinking ahead to your next special occasion—the office Christmas party or your sister's baby shower luncheon or perhaps an impromptu invitation to the new neighbors to come over for a let's-get-acquainted dinner. However the occasion is special to you, the food will match the moment.

FOR
FRIENDS
and
LOVERS

*I*n Graham Greene's postwar masterpiece *The End of the Affair*, the world-weary protagonist Maurice and his companion Sarah, who happens to be a friend's wife, share a grilled steak with onions at a crowded pub. Astonishingly innocent by today's standards of courtship, the scene was nevertheless adjudged so "romantic" that the novel was initially banned by British book censors. The reason given: the choice of foods was deemed too provocative.

Which just proves a point—good food has always been right at the top of the list of ways to win over a reluctant lover. It's regarded as a mood setter, an ice breaker, even an aphrodisiac. "Is it possible to fall in love over a plate of onions?" Maurice asks plaintively. "It seems improbable, and yet I could swear it was just then that I fell in love. . . ."

We're not about to suggest you invite your best friend's spouse out for a bite of steak and onions, but there are undoubtedly those moments in your own life when an evocative—perhaps even provocative—meal would push the right emotional buttons.

These special dishes can also set the mood for intimate celebrations of other kinds—dinners to deepen bonds with new friends, thirtieth birthday parties, or reunions with old chums, to name a few. With apologies to Graham Greene, romance is more than a plate of onions, and here are several starlit food ideas for pleasing friends and lovers.

Rick and Susie's Day at the Beach

YIELD: 4 TO 6 SERVINGS

Rick and Susie are an unusually matched pair—she is a world-class soprano, and he is a rural vet. Marriage for two such talented souls, Susie reports, is sometimes no day at the beach—but every now and then they kick up their heels and regain their balance with this wickedly good love potion.

NOTE: *We've given bar measurements here, with approximate cup measurements in parentheses.*

6 ounces (see note) vodka (¾ cup)
2 ounces grenadine (¼ cup)
4 ounces peach schnapps (½ cup)
4 ounces apple schnapps (½ cup)
16 ounces orange juice (2 cups)
2 ounces lemon juice (¼ cup)
8 ice cubes

1. Mix all ingredients in a blender until the ice is crushed and ingredients are well blended. Pour into wineglasses or tumblers and serve immediately.

Hot Chèvre Rounds with Basil and Sun-dried Tomatoes

YIELD: 3 TO 4 DOZEN ROUNDS

*I*n these wonderful little hors d'oeuvres, lightly toasted baguette slices are spread with a mild goat cheese and basil pesto, then crowned with sun-dried tomatoes. They're very simple and very pretty, and the red and green combination makes them just right for a Christmas party.

1 small (18 inches) baguette
1 (3-ounce) jar sun-dried tomatoes in olive oil
1 (8-ounce) log mild, creamy chèvre *or other goat cheese*
1 (3-ounce) jar (or, better yet, homemade) basil pesto

1. Preheat the oven to 375° F.

2. Cut the baguette into thin rounds. Place the rounds on a large ungreased baking sheet and toast them lightly in the oven for 3 to 5 minutes. Remove the sheet from the oven.

3. Raise the oven temperature to broil.

4. Drain and chop the tomatoes.

5. Spread the *chèvre* or other goat cheese on the toasted rounds. Spread a small spoonful of pesto over the cheese, and sprinkle the top with the chopped tomatoes.

6. Return the baking sheet to the oven and broil the toasts for 1 to 2 minutes. Serve immediately.

Chardonnay-Poached Salmon with Ginger and Three-Mustard Sauce

YIELD: 6 SERVINGS

*D*elicious though each might be, broiled chicken or roast tenderloin just doesn't have the right kind of dazzle for a romantic evening. This salmon dish has it. If you serve it cold, after doing the skinning, boning, and poaching, you can sit back and relax, knowing that dinner is ready to impress. And you won't have to cook a thing the next day, either; we've written the recipe to include an extra salmon steak and enough sauce to make the Summer Salmon Salad that follows.

THREE MUSTARD SAUCE:
½ cup coarse mustard (with seeds), such as Pommery
⅓ cup Dijon-style mustard
⅓ cup honey mustard
¼ cup lemon juice

SALMON:
2 cups water
1 cup Chardonnay
1 medium stalk celery
1 medium onion
½ teaspoon white peppercorns
2 bay leaves
1 tablespoon minced fresh ginger
6 (½-pound) salmon steaks (7 if making the following
   Summer Salmon Salad)

1. Combine all sauce ingredients in a small bowl. Set aside at room temperature. If making the summer salmon salad, reserve ½ cup of the sauce separately.

2. To poach the salmon, combine the water and wine in a fish poacher or a 10- to 12-inch sauté pan with a depth of 3 inches. Place the pan over high heat.

3. Slice the celery and onion into thin (⅛-inch) slices and add them to the pan with the peppercorns, bay leaves, and ginger. Bring the mixture to a boil, then lower the heat and simmer for 5 minutes.

Love: A word properly applied to our delight in particular kinds of food; sometimes metaphorically spoken of the favorite objects of all our appetites.

—Henry Fielding

4. Raise the heat to medium, then add the salmon steaks, and poach for 10 to 15 minutes. If the steaks are not completely submerged in the liquid, they must be turned after 7 minutes. If you are using a sauté pan rather than a fish poacher, you will probably need to poach the salmon in two batches. Skin and bone the first batch while the second is cooking.

5. When the salmon is done, skin and bone the steaks carefully, and arrange all 6 on a serving platter. (If you are making the summer salmon salad, refrigerate the seventh steak.) Serve the salmon immediately, topping with the sauce or passing it separately. Or chill well and serve cold. If you serve the salmon cold, allow the sauce to return to room temperature first.

Summer Salmon Salad

YIELD: 2 SERVINGS

*T*his recipe using leftovers from the Chardonnay-Poached Salmon with Ginger (see Index) dinner is perfect for a relaxed day-after-entertaining meal for two.

1 (½-pound) poached salmon steak, from Chardonnay-
   Poached Salmon with Ginger recipe
12 ounces red new potatoes (about 3 medium)
3 scallions
½ cup Three-Mustard Sauce, reserved from Chardonnay-
   Poached Salmon with Ginger recipe
¼ cup mayonnaise
1 tablespoon chopped fresh dill

1. Skin, bone, and flake the salmon. Place it in a medium bowl and set it aside.

2. Steam or boil the potatoes in their skins until tender, about 20 minutes. Cool and slice. You may remove the skins or leave them on, as you prefer.

3. Slice the scallions thinly (⅛-inch) on the bias. Add the potatoes and scallions to the salmon. Add the mustard sauce, mayonnaise, and dill and toss well to coat. Chill until ready to serve.

Martini Grilled Quail

YIELD: 2 SERVINGS

*T*he quail is indeed marinated in the ingredients of a well-mixed martini. The result is a bird that's, well, drunk with wonderful flavors. This romantic recipe will set aside any inhibition you might have about eating grilled quail with your fingers, as the experts do.

4 quail
2 tablespoons oil (unflavored, such as safflower, is best)
2 tablespoons dry vermouth
1 tablespoon gin
2 tablespoons tiny cocktail onions
1 tablespoon vinegar from the cocktail onions
1 teaspoon juniper berries (in the spice section of your supermarket)
Freshly ground pepper to taste

1. Split the quail through the backbone and flatten them. Place them breast-side up in an ungreased non-aluminum baking dish.

2. Combine the oil, vermouth, gin, cocktail onions and vinegar, juniper berries, and pepper in a small bowl. Pour the mixture over the quail. Turn the quail to coat them in the mixture, then cover and refrigerate to marinate overnight.

3. When ready to cook the quail, preheat the grill or broiler.

4. Remove the quail from the marinade and pat them dry with paper towels. Remove the onions from the marinade, if broiling.

5. If broiling, place the quail on a rack set over a baking sheet. Strew the onions over the quail and broil for 5 minutes per side, until golden brown. If grilling, grill the quail 5 minutes per side, brushing them with the marinade as they cook.

***RESULTS OF
YET ANOTHER WEE
UNSCIENTIFIC POLL TO
DETERMINE WHAT FOODS ARE
ROMANTIC***

♦ **Grilled steak for two**
♦ **Champagne for breakfast**
♦ **Cold fried chicken and a picnic with jonquils**
♦ **Ice-cream sundaes late at night**
♦ **Soufflés of any kind**
♦ **Freshly squeezed orange juice and a toasted muffin with lime marmalade**
♦ **Game hens with wild mushrooms**
♦ **Shirred eggs with marinated asparagus tips**
♦ **Crème brûlée**
♦ **Crêpes with melted chocolate sauce**

Chinatown Roast Duckling

YIELD: 4 SERVINGS

Most oriental duck recipes end up either too sweet or too spicy. This one has a nice balance and doesn't have an overpowering orange flavor.

4 large cloves garlic
1 tablespoon minced fresh ginger
2 (5- to 6-pound) ducklings, fresh or frozen and thawed
1 cup hoisin sauce
½ cup soy sauce
¼ cup honey
¼ cup orange juice

1. Preheat the oven to 425° F.

2. Mince the garlic. Combine the garlic and ginger in a small bowl.

3. Pull the fat pads from the duck cavities and discard, along with the packages of giblets inside the ducks. Rinse the ducks inside and outside and pat them dry. Place the ducks on a rack in a roasting pan. Using a sharp knife, prick the skin all over so that the excess fat can drain as the ducks cook.

4. Mix the hoison sauce, soy sauce, honey, and orange juice into the ginger-garlic mixture. Remove half the mixture to another small bowl and set aside.

5. Roast the ducks for 30 minutes.

6. Reduce the oven temperature to 350° F.

7. Brush the glaze from the first bowl over the ducks. Continue roasting the ducks at the lower temperature for another 1½ hours, basting intermittently with the glaze.

8. When ready to serve, carve the ducks and brush the slices with glaze from the reserved bowl.

Brandied Tenderloin with Bacon and Peppercorns

YIELD: 4 SERVINGS

*T*his recipe is perfect for a romantic dinner, and can be prepared several ways with a relatively small amount of work. The beef can be grilled or broiled, or even pan-fried in an iron skillet. We find that grilling and broiling are the simplest methods because the bacon cooks more easily and with less mess. It's delicious served with our Low Country Sweet Potatoes (see Index), which provide a soft and sweet contrast to the hot savory beef.

4 tenderloin steaks (6 to 8 ounces each)
4 slices bacon
1 tablespoon mixed peppercorns (pink, green, black and white; see note)
1 teaspoon dried thyme
2 tablespoons cognac
Salt to taste

NOTE: Available in specialty markets. If not available, a mixture of black and white will do.

1. Trim the steaks of any excess fat or gristle. Wrap a bacon slice around the edges of each steak. Secure with toothpicks and set aside.

2. Coarsely grind the peppercorns and mix them with the dried thyme in a small bowl. Press a scant ½ teaspoon of the peppercorn mixture into each side of the steaks. Place the steaks on a platter or baking dish.

3. Drizzle 1 tablespoon of the cognac over the top of the steaks. Turn the steaks and drizzle the other side with the remaining cognac. Cover and marinate the steaks for at least 2 hours, turning them occasionally. (If you will be marinating the steaks for longer than 2 hours, refrigerate them and bring them back to room temperature before cooking.)

4. Preheat a grill, griddle, or cast iron skillet over high heat or turn on the broiler.

5. Grill, panfry, or broil the steaks to the desired degree of doneness by searing each side, then lowering the temperature to finish cooking. Season the steaks to taste with the salt and serve.

Bourbon-Glazed Stuffed Pork Loin

YIELD: 6 TO 8 SERVINGS

When sliced and served, this dish gives off a romantic harvest aroma of meat and fruit. It's just the sort of thing to serve by the fireside in the fall. Carolina Carrots (recipe follows) are a perfect accompaniment.

STUFFING
6 ounces dried apricot slices
6 ounces dried pear slices
½ cup bourbon
½ cup water
1 boneless pork loin (approximately 3 pounds)
¼ pound shelled walnuts
2 tablespoons lemon juice

GLAZE:
2 tablespoons Dijon-style mustard
¼ cup honey
1 tablespoon lemon juice
¼ cup bourbon

1. Place the apricots, pears, bourbon, and water in a medium saucepan over high heat. Bring the mixture to a boil, then lower the heat and simmer, with the cover cracked, until the fruit is plump. Remove from the heat and let cool.

2. Preheat the oven to 350° F.

3. Untie the pork loin, if strung. Trim any surface fat and turn the loin upside down. Cut a slit the length of the roast, being careful not to cut through the bottom. Then, holding the knife flat, carefully cut through the middle of one side of the roast, being careful not to cut through the end. Repeat on the other side. Spread the meat open to butterfly and set aside.

4. Add the walnuts to the cooled fruit. Chop the fruit and walnuts together coarsely. Place the mixture in a medium bowl, add the lemon juice, and mix. Form the fruit and nuts into a loaf that will fit into the cavity you have just made in the pork.

5. Drape three pieces of string across a large roasting or baking pan. Place the stuffing loaf across the string and put the pork loin, cut-side down, over and around the stuffing. Tuck the sides under to re-form a roast, and tie the loin securely with the string.

6. To make the glaze, combine the mustard, honey, lemon juice, and bourbon in a small bowl and whisk until smooth.

7. Brush the surface of the loin generously with the glaze.

8. Roast the pork for approximately 1½ hours, brushing with the glaze every 30 minutes. Remove from the oven and let cool for 5 to 10 minutes before slicing. To serve, slice the loin starting at the short end, so that the stuffing shows in the middle of each slice.

Carolina Carrots

YIELD: 6 TO 8 SERVINGS

*F*resh cooked carrots are one of the most simple and delicious vegetables you can place on your table—yet unfortunately they are almost always overcooked by even the most well-meaning chefs. This lovely Carolina low-country recipe requires that you cook with a low, steady heat source to assure that the carrots remain firm and bursting with flavor.

1½ pounds carrots
1 scallion
2½ tablespoons butter
¼ teaspoon brown sugar
¼ teaspoon ground cinnamon
6 tablespoons water
1½ teaspoons chopped fresh mint
Salt and freshly ground pepper to taste

1. Trim the carrots. Cut into ¼-inch julienne strips. Trim and chop the scallion into ½-inch pieces.

2. Melt the butter in a heavy skillet over high heat. Add the chopped scallions and sauté for 2 minutes, just until softened. Add the julienned carrots, sugar, cinnamon, and water. Stir to combine. Cover and cook over low to moderate heat for 4 minutes.

3. Add the fresh mint. Continue cooking, covered, for about 15 minutes, until the carrots are tender, stirring occasionally. If all the water evaporates before the carrots are cooked, add 2 tablespoons more. Season with the salt and pepper and serve.

Mother's Warm Applesauce

YIELD: 6 TO 8 SERVINGS

A rugged New England friend of ours can't wait for the first crisp winds of autumn to arrive, for that's the traditional start of two of his favorite pastimes—chopping wood for the next year's winter and making his mother's recipe for warm applesauce. The recipe is so homey and good and nourishing, we can't think of anything better. Served cold or warm, it goes with everything from pancakes to pork roast and is delicious all by itself. We suggest you start your own applesauce-making tradition.

7 Granny Smith apples
zest of 2 lemons
1¼ cups water
2 tablespoons fresh lemon juice
½ cup sugar
⅔ cup sauternes
2 sticks cinnamon

1. Peel and quarter the apples. Core the apple quarters and cut them into irregular chunks. Set aside.

2. Grate the zest from the 2 lemons. Collect it in a small bowl and set it aside.

3. In a medium saucepan, combine the water, lemon juice, sugar, and sauternes.

4. Place the water mixture over high heat and bring it to a boil. Add the apple chunks, bring the mixture back to a boil, and lower heat to a brisk simmer. Cook, stirring often, for about 10 minutes, until the apples are tender.

5. Using a slotted spoon, remove the apples to a large bowl and mash them with a potato masher. Don't discard the syrup.

6. Add the cinnamon sticks to the remaining syrup in the saucepan. Bring the syrup to a boil and reduce it by half to two thirds. Remove the cinnamon sticks and whisk in the lemon zest. Drizzle the hot syrup over the apples.

SECRET PLEASURES

When M.F.K. Fisher asserts that "Almost every person has something secret he likes to eat," we think we know just what she means. Just ask any couple in love if don't they have foods that seem, well, just custom-made for them—anything from licorice-flavored jelly beans to black caviar pie. Knowing what someone most likes to eat is sometimes the most intimate kind of knowledge of all. Handled by the right pair of loving hands a little knowledge, as they say, can be a dangerous thing. Same goes for a tuna-noodle casserole.

Red Rufus Salad

YIELD: 4 SERVINGS

We named this salad for a genial friend of ours who prefers his salads—and everything else in his life, really—simple and sweet. To Rufus, life is one big juicy raspberry. So, we came up with a pretty pink salad that mingles full flavors and requires no last minute tossing. For the dressing, we like to use a raspberry wine that is produced in Vermont, but any good quality fruit wine will do nicely.

SALAD:
½ cup shelled walnuts
1 medium head red leaf lettuce
1 small red onion
1 large ripe pear (any variety, but Red Bartlett is best)

RASPBERRY WINE DRESSING:
1 cup raspberry wine (or other fruit wine)
2 tablespoons lemon juice
2 tablespoons sour cream
Salt and freshly ground pepper to taste

NOTE: The lettuce and onion can be prepared ahead of time (up to 1 hour), but do not slice the pear or sprinkle the walnuts on the salad until you're ready to serve—the pear will brown, and the walnuts will get soggy.

1. Preheat the oven to 300° F.

2. Chop the walnuts coarsely and spread them on an ungreased baking sheet. Toast them for 10 to 15 minutes, until well browned. Set aside to cool.

3. Reserve 4 large lettuce leaves and tear the rest into bite-sized pieces. Place the lettuce pieces in a large bowl and set aside.

4. Cut the onion into thin (⅛-inch or thinner) slices. Set aside.

5. Cut the unpeeled pear into thin (¼-inch) slices from stem to end.

6. Place all the dressing ingredients in a blender and blend until smooth.

7. Place the whole lettuce leaves on four salad plates. Add the onion slices to the lettuce pieces in the bowl and toss with just enough of the raspberry wine dressing to coat (about ¼ cup). Pile the lettuce and onion mixture onto each lettuce leaf. Place 4 or 5 pear slices in a fan pattern over the lettuce and onion. Sprinkle the toasted walnuts over the top. Pass the remaining dressing with the salad.

Caramel Pudding Cake

YIELD: 4 TO 6 SERVINGS

A talented cook we know informs us that she dreamed up this recipe to try to re-create a childhood memory for her husband. Actually, it was her guess that his dreams of a homemade classic were in fact of a certain Betty Crocker mix. The mix seems to be discontinued, but here is her marvelous effort to reproduce it—a homey but delicious pudding cake that her husband swears tastes better than the original.

CAKE:
½ tablespoon plus 4 tablespoons butter, softened
¾ cup sugar
2 tablespoons cold water
½ cup milk
½ teaspoon salt
1 teaspoon vanilla
1 cup flour
1 teaspoon baking powder

SAUCE:
½ cup sugar
2 tablespoons cold water
1 cup boiling water
½ cup brown sugar
1 teaspoon cornstarch
½ tablespoon cocoa
Vanilla ice cream or unsweetened whipped cream for topping

1. Preheat the oven to 350° F.

2. Butter an 8 × 8-inch baking pan. Set aside.

3. To make the cake, place ½ cup of the sugar with the cold water in a small heavy saucepan. Tilt the pan to wet all the sugar and place the pan over medium heat. As it heats, keep tilting the pan to even out the caramel. Continue cooking until the caramel is dark brown, but do not let it smoke much or it will burn. Remove the pan from the heat and let the caramel cool slightly. Standing back slightly (it will splatter), slowly whisk the milk into the caramel. (If the caramel was too cool when the milk was added, it will not dissolve properly. If this happens, return the pan to the heat for a minute or two to dissolve.) Set the mixture aside to cool.

4. In a medium mixing bowl, cream the softened butter with the remaining ¼ cup sugar, salt, and vanilla. In a separate small bowl, mix the flour and baking powder together. Add the cooled caramel to the butter mixture, then add the flour mixture and stir just to combine. Spread the batter into the prepared pan.

5. To make the sauce, make a caramel with the sugar and cold water as before: mix the sugar and cold water in a heavy saucepan and place over medium heat. Tilt to wet all the sugar and cook, continuing to tilt the pan to carmelize the sugar evenly. When it is golden brown, remove the pan from the heat. Stand slightly back, add the boiling water, and mix to dissolve. (There is no need to cool the caramel before adding the boiling water in this step.) Set aside.

6. In a separate bowl, mix the brown sugar, cornstarch, and cocoa. Slowly whisk in the caramel. Pour the sauce over the cake batter in the pan. Bake the pudding cake until a skewer comes out clean when inserted in the center of the cake, 35 to 40 minutes. Serve warm with vanilla ice cream or unsweetened whipped cream.

Godiva Hot Fudge Sauce

YIELD: ABOUT 1 CUP

A quick, easy, elegant topping that the world's leading chocolate experts provided for us. Wickedly good on Emma's Grand Marnier Ice Cream, Key West Sponge Cake (see Index for recipes), even fresh fruit.

3 ounces high-quality semisweet dark chocolate, preferably Godiva
2 eggs
1 cup sifted confectioners' sugar
1 tablespoon butter
1 tablespoon milk
1 teaspoon vanilla
2 tablespoons Grand Marnier

1. Melt the chocolate in a small heatproof bowl placed over a saucepan of simmering water. Add 1 egg and the sifted sugar and blend well with a spoon or whisk. Cook, stirring, until all the sugar is dissolved.

2. Add the second egg to the chocolate mixture. Beat well. Stir in the butter and milk. Continue cooking and stirring until the butter is melted and the sauce is well blended.

3. Remove the saucepan from the heat and stir in the vanilla and Grand Marnier.

4. Serve hot or at room temperature. Store, tightly covered, in the refrigerator.

THE BEST CHOCOLATE SHAKE EVER

The ultimate chocolate shake should be chocolaty but not syrupy, thick but with the taste of real milk. We've found that Godiva's Hot Fudge Sauce makes a milk shake that's just grand. Put four scoops of chocolate ice cream in a blender with 4 tablespoons Godiva Hot Fudge Sauce (cold), ½ cup milk, and 1 teaspoon vanilla extract. Blend just until smooth and serve immediately. Serves 2.

Two-Lime Mousse

*T*his romantic dessert conjures up harbor lights and languid Caribbean nights. It's creamy and slightly tart and looks elegant when served in a wineglass.

1 cup heavy cream, chilled
½ cup whipping cream, chilled
6 medium limes
1¼ cups sugar
1½ teaspoons flour
3 eggs
1 egg yolk
¼ cup Key lime juice (now commonly available in specialty markets and in some gourmet sections of supermarkets)
¼ teaspoon salt
½ cup boiling water
2 egg whites

1. Pour the heavy cream and whipping cream together into a large bowl. Beat them just until the cream begins to stiffen. (Not too stiff, or the cream will be too firm to fold into the mousse base and could turn to butter before you are finished, so watch carefully.) Refrigerate.

2. Set aside 1 lime for garnish. Grate the rind from as many limes as you need to obtain 2 tablespoons of grated rind. Squeeze the juice from 5 limes into a small bowl.

3. Mix the sugar and flour together in a medium heavy saucepan. Add the whole eggs and the egg yolk to the sugar-flour mixture and whisk well. Add the reserved lime juice, the Key lime juice, and the salt, and mix well.

4. Place the saucepan over medium heat. Add the boiling water, stirring continuously. Heat, stirring, just until the liquid begins to boil. Remove the saucepan from the heat and pour the mixture into a bowl. Let cool to lukewarm. (You may set the bowl over a pan of ice water and stir the mixture until it is cool, if you are in a hurry.) When the mixture is cool, whisk in the grated lime rind.

5. Place the egg whites in a medium bowl and beat them until they are firm, but not dry. Fold them into the lime base. Remove the whipped cream from the refrigerator and whisk it lightly to reblend. Remove and refrigerate ⅓ cup of the whipped cream for garnish. Using a spatula, carefully fold the remaining whipped cream into the lime base. Spoon the mousse into dessert cups, wineglasses, or one large dessert bowl and chill for at least 45 minutes.

6. When ready to serve, cut the reserved lime into 4 to 6 thick slices and halve the slices. Beat the reserved cream until stiff. Pipe or spoon a dollop onto each serving and top the whipped cream with a lime slice.

Coffee-Macadamia Freeze with Espresso Chocolate Sauce

YIELD: 4 SERVINGS

*T*his unusual dish was inspired by one of our consumer panelists who brought a Hawaiian coffee to a meeting for us to try—a brew flavored with macadamia nuts and a hint of chocolate. One thing led to another, and that led to a tantalizing dessert. This ultimate grown-up sundae is perfect for wooing someone with a sweet tooth.

MOUSSE:
¾ cup macadamia nuts
¾ cup heavy cream, chilled
½ cup freshly ground French Roast or Kona coffee beans
⅓ cup boiling water
1¼ teaspoons unflavored gelatin powder
4 tablespoons Armagnac
2 egg whites
4 egg yolks
½ cup sugar

ESPRESSO CHOCOLATE SAUCE:
4 ounces bittersweet chocolate
3 tablespoons espresso (freshly brewed or made from instant espresso)
3 tablespoons butter

1. Preheat the oven to 375° F.

2. Toast the macadamia nuts on a large ungreased baking sheet for 5 minutes, turning once with a metal spatula. Remove from the oven and let cool. Chop the toasted nuts and set them aside.

3. Pour the cream into a medium bowl and whip just until soft peaks begin to form. Refrigerate.

4. To make coffee, place ground coffee beans in a small bowl and pour the boiling water over them. Let the coffee steep for 3 minutes, then pour the mixture through a paper filter into a clean small bowl.

5. Sprinkle the gelatin over the strained coffee, add the Armagnac, and mix. Place the bowl in a saucepan of warm water. Place the pan over low heat and heat the coffee mixture, stirring, to melt the gelatin. Remove the pan from the heat.

6. Separate the eggs, placing the egg whites in a large bowl and the egg yolks in the bowl of an electric mixer. Set the yolks aside. Beat the egg whites until stiff and set aside.

7. Add the sugar to the egg yolks and beat at high speed until the mixture is thick and pale, and a wide ribbon of batter falls from the lifted beaters. Reduce the speed to slow and add the warm gelatin mixture slowly and gradually. Continue to beat just until the mixture is homogenous.

8. Fold the beaten egg whites and ½ cup of the chopped macadamia nuts into the egg yolk mixture. Reserve the rest of the chopped macadamia nuts to top the frozen mousse.

9. Remove the whipped cream from the refrigerator and whisk lightly to reblend. Using a spatula, fold the whipped cream into the yolk mixture. Pour the mousse into four ramekins, wineglasses, or other small serving cups (such as *pots de crème*) and place them in the freezer for 4 hours.

10. After 4 hours, place the mousse in the refrigerator to soften for about 30 minutes until ready to serve.

11. To make the sauce, place the chocolate and the espresso in a small heatproof bowl. Place the bowl in a medium saucepan of hot water, and place the pan over low heat. Add the butter and stir to melt.

12. To serve, pour the sauce over the chilled mousse and sprinkle with the remaining reserved chopped nuts.

THEME DINNER PARTIES

One of the things we've learned while catering dinner affairs of all sizes is that even the most accomplished and organized cooks get a wee bit nervous at the thought of producing a dinner party for, say, eight or ten discriminating guests.

We understand this stage fright completely. The ultimate challenge for any dinner host doubling as executive chef is to create the proper mood, serve the perfect meal, and have it all come together as effortlessly as if performed by a professional staff of ten.

The trick, we've discovered, is to start with a menu custom-made to the affair (a basic game plan, if you will), then work out preparation times, logistics, aesthetics, seating arrangements—in short, the little things that can drive an ambitious host crazy. In this chapter we offer five basic menus that cover a range of seasonal and social possibilities: a tidewater supper, an autumn equinox dinner, a country French supper, a festive summer fete, and a classic Mediterranean menu.

These carefully selected menus are guaranteed to win you the unstinting admiration of your dinner guests. More important for you, though, each menu's preparation time has been geared to keeping you where the important action is taking place—playing the charming (and sane) dinner host.

TIDEWATER SUPPER

Virginia Gentleman ♦ and spring water

Mason-Dixon Croutons

Country Ham with Crab and Cider

Tidewater Rice

Carolina Carrots

Mother's Warm Applesauce

Godiva Angel Pie

Coffee

♦ the only bourbon made in Virginia

Mason-Dixon Croutons

YIELDS: 24 CROUTONS (6 TO 8 SERVINGS)

*I*n this recipe, toasted pumpkin seeds are ground and combined with Key lime juice, curry powder, and mayonnaise to make a magnificent spread that is broiled on thin slices of French bread and served hot. Your guests will spend a lot of time both eating the marvelous croutons and trying their best to think what it is that they taste like.

8 ounces hulled pumpkin seeds (available in health food stores)
1 (18-inch) baguette
⅓ cup mayonnaise
4 tablespoons Key lime juice
1 teaspoon curry powder
Salt and freshly ground pepper to taste

1. Preheat the oven to 350° F.

2. Toast the pumpkin seeds on an ungreased baking sheet for 7 minutes, until well browned. Remove and let cool.

3. Cut the baguette into twenty-four ½-inch slices. Spread the slices on the baking sheet and toast them lightly in the oven, for about 5 minutes. Remove and let cool.

4. Raise the oven temperature to broil.

5. Place the toasted pumpkin seeds in the bowl of a food processor fitted with a steel blade. Process to grind (but watch carefully and process in short pulses—they should be finely chopped, rather than completely ground. If they are ground too fine, they will get oily). Remove the chopped seeds to a medium bowl.

6. Add the mayonnaise, lime juice, curry powder, salt, and pepper to the chopped pumpkin seeds. Mix well.

7. Spread the pumpkin seed mixture on one side of the toasted French bread slices. Place them in the oven and broil them just until they are lightly browned and heated through. Serve immediately.

Country Ham and Crab with Cider

YIELD: 6 SERVINGS

A Southern gentleman friend of ours developed this recipe from his memory of a spectacular meal he had long ago in the famous dining room of the Hotel Roanoke in Roanoke, Virginia. Even the most daring gourmands would think twice before combining the distinctive flavors of country ham and crab, although both are basic to the Southern way of eating. Somehow the gentling influence of the sweet cider ties them together beautifully.

Country ham is a dry-cured ham, like a Smithfield, that is very salty. Poaching in the cider both tenderizes the meat and reduces the saltiness.

6 country ham steaks, 1/4-inch thick
3 cups cider (1 1/2 pints)
1 1/2 pounds fresh crabmeat (do not substitute frozen)

1. Preheat the oven to 325° F.

2. Arrange the ham steaks in one layer in a large roasting pan or jelly roll pan. Pour the cider over the ham to cover.

3. Bake the ham, uncovered, for about 30 minutes, or until tender. Do not allow the ham to get dry; or it will become tough. Keep the steaks covered by adding more cider if necessary.

4. While the ham bakes, fill a medium saucepan with water and bring it to a boil. Place the crabmeat in a steamer. Five minutes before serving, place the steamer over the boiling water, cover, and steam the crab for 5 minutes to heat through.

5. To serve, place the ham steaks on individual serving dishes. Top each steak with a mound of crabmeat and drizzle the crab lightly with the cider drippings. Serve immediately.

Tidewater Rice

YIELD: 6 TO 8 SERVINGS

A marvelous dinner companion for Country Ham and Crab with Cider, this dish also goes well with any kind of grilled seafood or chicken—even with a brunch omelet.

3 slices bacon
1 pound smoked sausage, such as kielbasa
½ small red onion
1 medium stalk celery
½ small green bell pepper
½ small red or yellow bell pepper
1 small clove garlic
1 cup long grain brown rice
¼ cup wild rice, or ½ cup mixed wild and brown rice
1 cup plus 6 tablespoons water
½ cup molasses
Salt and freshly ground pepper to taste

1. Heat a heavy skillet over medium heat. Place the bacon slices in the hot pan and fry until crisp. Remove bacon and set aside to drain on paper towels.

2. Drain all but 2 tablespoons of the bacon fat from the skillet. Set the skillet aside.

3. Slice the sausage into ⅓- to ¼-inch-thick slices and set aside. Chop the red onion into ⅓-inch dice. Chop the celery into ¼-inch dice. Chop the peppers into ⅓-inch dice. Crush the garlic clove with the side of a knife.

4. Return the skillet to medium heat. Add the sliced sausage, the diced onion, celery, and peppers, and the garlic clove to the skillet. Sauté for 10 minutes, stirring often with a wooden spoon.

5. Rinse and drain the uncooked rices, then add them with the water and molasses to the skillet. Stir and bring to a boil. Lower the heat, cover the skillet, and simmer the rice for 45 minutes to 1 hour, until the rice is tender and all the liquid is absorbed.

6. Season with salt and pepper to taste. Crumble the reserved bacon over the top of the serving dish and serve.

Fill a large bowl with colorful shells, or with a mixture of clean white sand and shells, and use it for a centerpiece.

Decorate with dried reeds, cattails, and other tall, natural grasses.

Tie colorful cotton dish-towels with contrasting ribbon and use them as oversized napkins, or lay them flat and use as cotton placemats.

Godiva Angel Pie

YIELD: 1 (8-INCH) PIE

Godiva Chocolates dreamed up this elegant version of the chocolate cream pie you adored as a child. It can be enhanced with any number of the "adult" accents included here—fresh raspberries in cream, Chocolate-Pecan Cream, bourbon-flavored cream, cocoa dusting, or strawberries marinated in California champagne.

MERINGUE SHELL:
1 teaspoon butter
1 cup pecan halves
2 egg whites
½ cup sugar
⅛ teaspoon salt
½ teaspoon vanilla

CHOCOLATE FILLING:
1 cup heavy cream, chilled
4 ounces semisweet dark chocolate, preferably Godiva
3 tablespoons water
1 teaspoon vanilla
Raspberry Cream, Whipped Bourbon Cream, Cocoa Stencil, Chocolate-Pecan Cream, or Sliced Strawberries in Champagne for garnish.

1. Preheat the oven to 300° F.

2. Using 1 teaspoon of butter, lightly butter an 8-inch pie plate.

3. To make the meringue shell, chop the pecan halves finely.

4. In a large bowl, beat the egg whites until they are firm, but not dry. Sprinkle the sugar, salt, vanilla, and nuts over the surface of the egg whites, then fold everything together using a spatula or flat spoon.

5. Spoon the meringue mixture into the buttered pie plate. Using the back of a spoon, form a nest-like shell and build the sides up ½ inch above the edge of the pan.

6. Bake the shell for 35 to 40 minutes, until golden brown. Remove from the oven and cool.

7. To make the filling, pour the cream into a large bowl and beat it just until soft peaks begin to form. Refrigerate.

8. Place the chocolate and the water in a medium heatproof bowl. Set the bowl over a saucepan of simmering water. Heat, stirring, until the chocolate is melted.

9. When the chocolate is melted, remove the bowl from the heat, add the vanilla and whisk lightly. Set aside to cool until slightly thickened (3 to 5 minutes).

10. Remove the whipped cream from the refrigerator and whisk lightly to reblend. Whisk one third of the whipped cream, a spoonful at a time, into the melted chocolate, incorporating each spoonful completely before adding the next. Fold the remaining two thirds of the whipped cream into the mixture.

11. Pile the filling into the meringue shell. Smooth the surface with a spatula, and chill 4 to 5 hours, or until firm. Just before serving, garnish one of the following ways.

Raspberry Cream

⅓ cup heavy cream, chilled
1 small box (½ pint) fresh raspberries

1. Pour the cream into a medium bowl and beat until stiff. Fit a pastry bag with a star tip, fill the bag with the whipped cream, and pipe a border of simple rosettes around the edge of the pie.

2. Top each rosette with a fresh raspberry.

Whipped Bourbon Cream

⅓ cup heavy cream, chilled
2 tablespoons bourbon

1. Pour the cream into a medium bowl and beat until soft peaks begin to form.

2. Add the bourbon to the whipped cream and beat until stiff.

3. Spoon a dollop of bourbon cream over each serving of pie.

Cocoa Stencil

2 tablespoons cocoa
2 tablespoons confectioners' sugar

1. Using a colander or sifter, sift the cocoa over the entire surface of the pie.

2. Place a stencil or doily lightly over the cocoa. Sift the confectioners' sugar over the stencil. Carefully remove the stencil and serve immediately.

Chocolate-Pecan Cream

½ cup heavy cream, chilled
¼ cup pecan halves
1 ounce semisweet dark chocolate, preferably Godiva

1. Preheat the oven to 350° F.

2. Pour the cream into a medium bowl and beat just until soft peaks begin to form. Refrigerate.

3. Spread the pecans on an ungreased baking sheet and toast for 5 to 7 minutes, until well browned. Remove from the oven, cool, and then chop coarsely.

4. When ready to serve, cut the pie and place a piece on each serving plate. Whisk the cream lightly to reblend and spoon it over the top and edges of each piece. Sprinkle the chopped pecans over the cream. Using a vegetable peeler, shave some chocolate over each serving.

Sliced Strawberries in Champagne

1 pint fresh strawberries, hulled
¾ cup California champagne
1 teaspoon sugar

1. Slice the hulled strawberries and place them in a medium bowl. Pour the champagne over the strawberries, sprinkle with the sugar, and marinate for 30 minutes before serving.

2. When ready to serve, drain the strawberries well and spoon some over each serving.

Morel Roulades

YIELD: 6 LUNCHEON SERVINGS; 8 TO 10 APPETIZER PORTIONS

Sliced thinly, these roulades (fancy roll-ups) are splendid starters for an autumn Equinox dinner. They are deli-
cately flavored with sherry and nutmeg, and are filled with
a creamy sauce of morels, mushrooms, ham, and garlic.
Sliced a wee bit thicker, they make a great brunch with an
accompanying salad, or perfectly complement a roasted
game bird for dinner.

FILLING:
1 ounce dried morels
1 pound fresh mushrooms
2 large cloves garlic
½ pound cooked lean ham (sliced ¼ inch thick)
2 tablespoons butter
Salt and freshly ground pepper to taste
2 tablespoons sherry or Madeira
½ cup heavy cream
1 ounce cream cheese
¼ cup chopped fresh parsley

ROULADE:
Oil for pan
6 eggs
1 egg white
½ teaspoon salt
½ teaspoon freshly ground white pepper
½ teaspoon ground nutmeg
2 tablespoons sherry or Madeira
3 tablespoons flour

1. To make the filling, place the morels in a small bowl,
and pour enough hot water over them to cover. Let them
stand for 20 minutes.

2. Meanwhile, chop the mushrooms. Mince the garlic.
Dice the ham.

3. Drain the morels, reserving the liquid. Remove and
discard the stems of the morels. Wash the rest carefully
under running water, inside and out, to remove all traces
of sand and dirt. Chop the cleaned morels. Strain the
reserved soaking liquid through cheesecloth or a fine-
meshed colander. Set it aside.

AN AUTUMN
EQUINOX DINNER

Dry Sherry

Morel Roulades

Hazelnut-Baked Pork
Chops

Yankee Griddle Corn
Cakes

Mixed Greens and Cana-
dian Bacon

Pumpkin Ginger Cheese-
cake

Coffee

---

4. Melt the butter in a large skillet over high heat. Add the regular mushrooms, salt, and pepper. Toss to coat with butter. Cook, stirring occasionally, until the mushrooms have exuded their liquid (about 3 to 5 minutes). Add the reserved soaking liquid and continue to cook until the liquid evaporates and the mushrooms brown slightly.

5. Add the morels and cook for 1 minute. Add the garlic and cook another minute, then add the diced ham and toss. Stir in the sherry or Madeira, cream, and cream cheese, then lower the heat to medium and stir to melt the cheese. Cook, stirring, until the mushrooms and ham are coated. Add the chopped parsley and remove the filling from the heat.

6. Preheat the oven to 375° F.

7. To make the roulade, lightly oil a jelly roll pan and line it with wax paper. Lightly oil the paper as well.

8. Separate the eggs, placing yolks in one large bowl and whites in another. Add the extra egg white to the other 6 egg whites. Set the whites aside.

9. Add the salt, pepper, and nutmeg to the egg yolks. Beat them until they are thick and pale. Add the sherry or Madeira and continue to beat until the egg yolks are very thick and almost white.

10. Slowly blend the flour into the egg yolk mixture.

11. Beat the egg whites until they are firm but not dry. Using a spatula, fold the beaten egg whites into the yolk mixture.

12. Spread the batter in an even layer in the prepared pan. Place the roulade in the oven to bake for 12 to 15 minutes, until puffed and slightly browned.

13. Remove the pan from the oven and let it cool for 2 minutes, then invert it on a large sheet of wax paper. Gently remove the oiled wax paper from what is now the top of the roulade. Spread the mushroom filling in an even layer over the roulade. Roll it up carefully, starting from the long side. Place the roulade, seam-side down, on a cutting board. Cut it into ½-inch slices and serve immediately.

Use paper leaves (available in specialty shops and many mail order companies) to garnish plates—place them under hors d'oeuvre trays or any other serving dish for finger food.

Fill a basket with shiny gourds and dried flowers, or with acorns you've collected. Place a miniature pumpkin or tiny gourd at each place setting.

Hazelnut-Baked Pork Chops

YIELD: 6 TO 8 SERVINGS

*T*his menu is a wonderful way to welcome fall. Or try serving these pork chops with red cabbage and baked apples and perhaps a wedge of fresh cider bread—this is an ideal dish to share with close friends on a crisp fall evening.

1 cup shelled hazelnuts (or substitute walnuts or pecans)
2 large cloves garlic
⅓ cup coarse mustard (with seeds), such as Pommery
¼ cup Dijon-style mustard
¼ cup dry white wine, such as Chardonnay
2 tablespoons chopped fresh Italian parsley
½ cup dry, unseasoned bread crumbs
8 pork chops (½ to ¾ inch thick)
Salt and freshly ground pepper to taste
2 tablespoons olive or peanut oil
1½ tablespoons butter, melted

1. Grind the hazelnuts coarsely in a blender or food processor fitted with a steel blade.

2. Mince the garlic finely and place it in a small bowl.

3. Add both of the mustards and the wine to the garlic and blend.

4. On a flat pan or large plate, mix the ground hazelnuts with the chopped parsley and bread crumbs.

5. Trim the pork chops of fat and sprinkle them with salt and pepper to taste.

6. Heat the olive or peanut oil in a large sauté pan over medium-high heat. Sear the chops on both sides. Remove from the heat.

7. Preheat the oven to 375° F.

8. Brush the seared chops with the mustard mixture, then press both sides into the hazelnut mixture to coat.

9. Place the chops on a large flat baking pan. Drizzle them with the melted butter. Bake them until the topping is crispy and the chops are juicy but cooked through, about 15 to 20 minutes.

We serve toasted nuts on dozens of things: melted Brie, winter soups, cold pasta salads, and ice-cream desserts, to name just a few. Therefore we always keep a hearty supply of nuts on hand—macadamias, black walnuts, cashews, almonds, and big Georgia peanuts are our favorites.

Yankee Griddle Corn Cakes

YIELD: 6 SERVINGS

*I*t's funny how many people are inclined to think of traditional griddle cakes as only breakfast fare. They're certainly a natural for that—especially when served with real maple syrup or a liberal scoop of Mother's Warm Applesauce (see Index). But consider also making these satisfying cakes as an unexpected side dish for a flavorful dinner roast or some other kind of hearty weekend menu. We've paired them here with hazelnut-baked pork chops, for a robust autumn meal.

1 slice bacon
1 egg
1¼ cups buttermilk
2 tablespoons corn or vegetable oil
¼ cup flour
½ teaspoon baking soda
1 teaspoon baking powder
1 teaspoon sugar
½ teaspoon salt
¾ cup cornmeal

1. In a heavy skillet or griddle, cook the bacon over low heat until crisp. Remove to drain on a paper towel. When cool, crumble and set aside. Pour the melted fat from the griddle into a small bowl and reserve.

2. Heat the griddle slowly to medium-hot.

3. In a medium bowl, beat the egg lightly with a whisk. Add the buttermilk, oil, and reserved bacon fat. Whisk until well blended.

4. In a separate medium bowl, sift together the flour, baking soda, baking powder, sugar, and salt. Mix in the cornmeal.

5. Make a well in the flour mixture. Add the egg-buttermilk mixture along with the crumbled bacon. Mix everything together just to combine.

6. Pour scant ¼ cup portions onto the hot griddle and cook until bubbles completely cover the tops of the cakes. Turn and brown the second side. Serve hot with butter.

Mixed Greens and Canadian Bacon

YIELD: 6 SERVINGS

When you dive into this bundle of nutritious greens—collards, turnip greens, and spinach—you can just feel the vitamins pumping through your veins. The Canadian bacon adds a smoky flavor without adding a lot of unnecessary fat.

1 medium bunch fresh collard greens
1/2 large bunch turnip or dandelion greens
1 (10-ounce) bag fresh spinach
6 thick slices Canadian bacon
1 tablespoon butter
1/4 cup cider vinegar

1. Discard the stems from the collard greens, turnip greens, and spinach leaves. Wash all the greens well (do not dry) and tear them into bite-sized pieces.

2. Cut the Canadian bacon into 1/3-inch strips.

3. Melt the butter in a large skillet over medium-high heat. Add the bacon strips and toss to brown them lightly. Add the collard greens and cover the skillet. Steam them for approximately 5 minutes, then uncover the skillet and add the turnip greens. Re-cover the skillet and steam the greens for another 3 minutes. Uncover the skillet again and add the spinach leaves. Re-cover the skillet and steam the greens for another 2 minutes.

4. When all the greens have been steamed, uncover the skillet and pour the cider vinegar over the greens and Canadian bacon. Toss and serve immediately.

A FEW GREEN LEAVES

BEET TOPS

Also called beet greens, they are available in the spring and early summer. The stems are dark red and taste slightly of beets, and the leaves are rich, dark green, and mild.

COLLARDS

A Southern favorite, available in most produce sections year-round. Traditionally cooked with salt pork or ham; we like them with Canadian bacon and cider or cranberry vinegar.

MUSTARD GREENS

A stronger-flavored green. We like to serve them fresh, mixed in a salad with one or two other fresh greens. Good in a salad with endive, toasted pine nuts, and a light mustard vinaigrette.

SWISS CHARD

A close cousin in taste to beet greens, with a little less mild flavor. Try serving chard cooked, chopped, and well drained in a Swiss Chard Eggs Florentine—a poached egg with smoked ham on a bed of chard over a toasted English muffin, topped with a creamy Gorgonzola cheese sauce.

Pumpkin-Ginger Cheesecake

YIELD: 8 TO 10 SERVINGS

When Thanksgiving rolls around, we just can't seem to keep enough of these cheesecakes in our stores. The company that makes them for us wouldn't part with its secret recipe, so we had to devise our own to provide for those hungry souls who might have missed it every year. (They sell out fast.) Don't be daunted by the idea of baking a cheesecake—the spectacular results make it look a lot more difficult than it really is. Our recipe requires only about thirty minutes' worth of work. The rest is baking and chilling time. A wonderful autumn dessert twist.

GINGER CRUMB CRUST:
3 tablespoons butter
¾ cup graham cracker crumbs
½ cup crushed gingersnaps
1 tablespoon brown sugar
1 teaspoon ground cinnamon

FILLING:
½ cup heavy cream, chilled
1 (3-ounce) and 2 (8-ounce) packages cream cheese, softened
1 cup sugar
2 large eggs
1 cup cooked, mashed pumpkin, canned or fresh
½ teaspoon ground cinnamon
½ teaspoon powdered ginger
¼ teaspoon ground cloves
¼ cup pecan halves

1. Preheat the oven to 350° F.

2. To make the crust, place the butter in a small saucepan and melt over moderate heat. While the butter is melting, mix the graham cracker crumbs, gingersnaps, brown sugar, and cinnamon in a medium bowl. Add the melted butter and mix together with a fork.

3. Press the crumb mixture into the bottom and sides of a 10-inch springform pan. Bake for 10 minutes, then remove from the oven and let cool.

4. Reduce the oven temperature to 300° F.

5. To make the filling, pour the heavy cream into a medium bowl and beat just until soft peaks form. Refrigerate.

6. In a large bowl, beat the cream cheese with an electric mixer until fluffy. Gradually add the sugar, beating well. Add the eggs one at a time, and beat the mixture until it is fluffy, pale, and homogenous. Stir in the pumpkin, cinnamon, ginger, and cloves.

7. Remove the whipped cream from the refrigerator and whisk lightly to reblend. Using a spatula or flat spoon, fold the whipped cream into the cream cheese-pumpkin mixture. Pour the mixture into the prepared crust and bake for 1 hour, until firm.

8. Cool the cheesecake to room temperature, then refrigerate for at least 3 hours to chill thoroughly. Remove the sides of the springform pan. Just before serving, place the pecan halves on top of the cheesecake, in a ring around the edges, to garnish.

Smoked Oyster Toasts
with Herb Butter

YIELD: ABOUT 2 DOZEN

*T*he simplest appetizers are often the best. Here's an easy start for a classic French supper. We prefer to use smoked oysters, but you can use fresh ones with good results. You may also wish to try serving the herb toasts with a chicken liver pâté or mild cheese. They're a zesty alternative to plain crackers.

HERB BUTTER:
1 large clove garlic
6 tablespoons butter, softened
2 tablespoons extra virgin olive oil
2 tablespoons chopped fresh Italian parsley
2 tablespoons snipped fresh chives
½ teaspoon dried thyme
Salt and freshly ground pepper to taste

OYSTER TOASTS:
1 narrow (2-inch) loaf French bread
1 can smoked oysters, drained (see note)

NOTE: For fresh oyster toasts, use the same recipe but toast the bread plain on both sides first, then spread it with the herb butter, place 1 oyster on each toast, and top each with an additional dollop of butter. Broil the toasts and oysters in a preheated broiler for 2 minutes and serve immediately.

1. Preheat the oven to 400° F.

2. Mince the garlic.

3. Place the softened butter in a small bowl and beat it until it is creamy. Add the olive oil, parsley, chives, thyme, garlic, and salt and pepper. Mix well.

4. Cut the bread into ⅓-inch slices. Spread the herb butter onto one side of all the slices and place them in a layer on a large ungreased baking sheet. Toast them in the oven for 5 minutes, until golden and slightly crisp. Top each slice with 1 or 2 smoked oysters and serve immediately. (If guests are serving themselves, you may want to place the herb toasts on a platter next to a bowl of the smoked oysters, and they may put them on themselves.)

A FRENCH
COUNTRY SUPPER

Pouilly-Fumé

Smoked Oyster Toasts with
Herb Butter

Veal Chops with Special
Cognac Sauce

Zinfandel

Wild Blue Salad

Sage-Roasted Potatoes

Wedding Cake Sorbet with
Champagne

Café au lait

Veal Chops with Special Cognac Sauce

YIELD: 4 SERVINGS

*T*his is an elegant dinner party recipe—relatively fast and easy, sophisticated, and filled with robust French flavors. The nutty crunch and apple tartness are beautifully balanced by the cognac and cider.

¼ cup shelled pistachios (about 2 ounces in the shell)
2 medium tart apples, such as Granny Smith
2 tablespoons butter
2 tablespoons vegetable oil
4 veal chops (rib or loin chops, about 1 inch thick)
Salt and freshly ground pepper to taste
3 tablespoons cognac
1⅓ cups apple cider or apple juice
2 tablespoons lemon juice

1. Chop the pistachios coarsely and set them aside.

2. Peel, quarter, and core the apples. Cut them lengthwise into ¼-inch slices. Cut the slices lengthwise again in thirds.

3. In a large sauté pan, melt the butter over high heat. Add the apple and brown, tossing often until barely tender (4 to 5 minutes). Remove the apple slices and set them aside.

4. Add the vegetable oil to the sauté pan and return it to the heat. Sear the chops in the hot oil for 1 to 2 minutes on each side, until browned. Reduce the heat to medium and continue cooking the chops, turning occasionally, for 15 to 20 minutes, until pink but still juicy. Remove the chops to a serving platter. Sprinkle with salt and pepper to taste.

5. Pour off the excess fat from the sauté pan and return it to the heat. When the pan is hot, deglaze it by pouring in the cognac, the apple cider or apple juice, and the lemon

juice. Bring the liquid to a boil, stirring. Continue boiling until the liquid is reduced to about 1 cup (5 to 7 minutes).

6. Salt the sauce to taste. Reheat the apples by adding them to the pan and heating them with the liquid for 1 to 2 minutes.

7. Remove the pan from the heat. Spoon the hot sauce over the chops on the serving platter. Sprinkle with the pistachios and serve immediately.

Wild Blue Salad

YIELD: 4 SERVINGS

*T*he key to this intriguing salad is the Bavaria Blue cheese, a soft, creamy cheese that can be found at most good markets these days. Another creamy blue cheese, such as Blue Castello or Saga Blue, will also give it the same heady flavor. An elegant first course that also makes a nice, light take-along lunch.

6 ounces Bavaria Blue, or other soft, creamy blue cheese
1½ pounds fresh spinach
1 cup red radishes
¾ cup walnut pieces (halves or broken bits)
¼ cup walnut oil
¼ cup olive oil
2 tablespoons white wine vinegar or lemon juice
½ teaspoon dry mustard
Salt and freshly ground pepper to taste

1. Trim the rind from the cheese. Place the trimmed cheese in the freezer for 25 to 30 minutes to firm it for easier cutting.

2. Remove and discard the stems from the spinach. Wash the leaves well and pat or spin them dry.

3. Cut the radishes into ¼-inch slices.

4. Combine the spinach, radish slices, and walnut pieces in a serving bowl.

5. Place all the remaining ingredients in a blender and blend until smooth. Set aside.

6. Remove the cheese from the freezer and cut it into ¼- to ½-inch dice. (This is easiest to do by first slicing the cheese lengthwise, then cutting the slices into sticks, and then the sticks into dice.) Add the diced cheese to the spinach mixture.

7. Pour the dressing over the salad, toss, and serve.

Sage-Roasted Potatoes

YIELD: 4 TO 6 SERVINGS

We developed this accompaniment dish with this special occasion French dinner in mind. Then our clever recipe tester served it one morning with scrambled eggs, and there went all our hotshot planning. Well, perhaps you should be the judge of when—and with what—to serve these versatile potatoes.

2½ pounds medium red potatoes
3 tablespoons butter
2 teaspoons dried sage (try marjoram some time)
Salt and freshly ground pepper to taste

1. Preheat the oven to 350° F.

2. Wash and quarter the potatoes.

3. Place the butter in a roasting pan and melt it in the oven or over a burner until very hot.

4. Add the quartered potatoes to the hot pan and stir to coat with the butter. Sprinkle with the sage, salt, and pepper.

5. Roast, stirring occasionally, for 1 hour, or until lightly browned and soft when pierced with skewer.

Wedding Cake Sorbet with Champagne

YIELD: 4 SERVINGS

We know a single man who is wild about this festive dessert. It's a pure white sorbet embellished with candied violets and surrounded by a moat of champagne. The sorbet tastes a little bit like wedding cake frosting—frilly, with a strong vanilla accent. You may top it with fresh raspberries or sliced peaches. A single friend reports that when he eats this dessert, all sort of inspired ideas seem possible to him—even matrimony.

2 cups water
1 cup sugar
1 tablespoon vanilla
2 egg whites
¼ teaspoon cream of tartar
¼ teaspoon salt
1 teaspoon grated lemon rind
1 cup champagne (not too dry)
8 to 12 candied violets

1. Bring the water and sugar to a boil in a medium heavy saucepan over high heat. Reduce the heat to medium and cook the syrup for 5 minutes; then remove the pan from the heat and let the syrup cool. When the syrup is luke-warm, add the vanilla and place the pan in the freezer to chill quickly.

2. When chilled, pour the syrup into an ice cream freezer and churn according to manufacturer's directions, until almost frozen.

3. While the sorbet is churning, place the egg whites in a medium bowl and beat them until soft peaks begin to form. Add the cream of tartar and salt and continue to beat until the whites are firm but not dry.

4. When the sorbet is almost frozen, transfer it to a large bowl. Using a spatula, fold the beaten egg whites and the lemon rind into the sorbet. Transfer the sorbet to an 8-inch cake pan and return it to the freezer for about 2 hours, until completely frozen.

5. When ready to serve, mound a high peak in each of four serving glasses or dishes. Pour ¼ cup champagne around the sorbet at the base (like a moat). Decorate with candied violets and serve immediately.

Spiced Fruit Soup

YIELD: 4 TO 6 SERVINGS

*T*his chilled soup is ideally suited for the first course of a grand summer fete. It's an unusual fruit soup in that it isn't cream-based—therefore, it's considerably less filling, has fewer calories, and seems less like a dessert. And the spices are an unexpected touch of holiday flavor in July.

2 medium oranges
3 cups orange juice
½ cup lemon juice
1 tablespoon plus ¼ cup sugar
2 teaspoons cornstarch
Pinch of salt
2 sticks cinnamon
¼ teaspoon ground cloves
1 large nectarine
1 medium peach
2 tablespoons flour
3 tablespoons Cointreau
1 small seedless orange for garnish

1. Using a sharp paring knife, peel the oranges. Cut the sections from the membranes over a bowl to catch the juices. Place the orange sections in the bowl with the juices. Squeeze all the juice from the remaining pulp into the bowl and discard the pulp. Remove and discard any seeds. Cover the bowl and set it aside.

2. In a large saucepan, combine the orange juice, lemon juice, and 1 tablespoon of the sugar with the cornstarch, salt, cinnamon sticks, and cloves. Over high heat, bring the liquid to a boil, then lower the heat to medium-low and simmer for 5 to 10 minutes.

3. While the soup is simmering, pit and chop the unpeeled nectarine and peach. Place them in a medium bowl and sprinkle the remaining ¼ cup sugar and the flour over them. Toss to coat.

4. After the soup has simmered for 5 to 10 minutes, add the nectarine-peach mixture to the saucepan. Return the soup to a boil, stirring. Lower the heat again and simmer for 5 minutes longer. Remove the pan from the heat and let the soup cool. Stir the reserved orange sections and juice, along with the Cointreau, into the soup. Chill thoroughly in the refrigerator.

5. When ready to serve, cut the seedless orange into thin slices. Spoon the soup into bowls and float an orange slice on each serving.

Seafood Salad with Tropical Fruits

YIELD: 4 SERVINGS

*T*his salad is short on bother and long on elegance. It's a perfect dish for outdoor summer entertaining, because you can balance it easily on your lap, and you only need a fork. The vinaigrette will keep for up to two weeks in the refrigerator, so you may want to make extra; it's delicious on simple green salads and makes a nice marinade for either meat or seafood.

BURGUNDY VINAIGRETTE:
½ medium onion
1 medium clove garlic
¼ cup white burgundy or other Chardonnay
1½ tablespoons white wine vinegar
1 tablespoon Dijon-style mustard
1 tablespoon coarse mustard (with seeds), such as Pommery
1 cup peanut oil
⅓ cup walnut oil
Salt and freshly ground pepper to taste

SALAD:
1 small head red leaf lettuce, or other leafy green, such as Boston, romaine, or arugula
5 ounces fresh spinach (½ 10-ounce bag)
½ pound fresh halibut (you may substitute fresh perch, salmon, or sole, but the poaching time must be changed accordingly)
½ pound fresh scallops
16 fresh medium shrimp, uncooked
1 small cantaloupe or honeydew melon
1 medium papaya
1 small pineapple
¼ pound buckwheat noodles

1. Make the dressing first. Mince the onion and garlic and place them together in a blender. Add all the remaining ingredients and blend well.

2. Refrigerate the vinaigrette until it is ready to use.

3. Wash and dry the lettuce and tear it into small pieces. Place the pieces in a large bowl.

4. Discard the stems from the spinach. Wash the leaves well, pat them dry, and add them to the lettuce. Refrigerate.

5. Fill a sauté pan with water to a depth of 2 to 3 inches. Place the pan over high heat and bring the water to a boil. Lower the heat to a simmer. Poach the halibut in the simmering water for 5 to 7 minutes, until it is firm and completely opaque. (Poach sole for 2 to 3 minutes, salmon for 5 to 7 minutes, and perch for 3 to 5 minutes.) Remove the halibut with a slotted spoon and place it on a plate to cool. Keep the water simmering.

6. While the halibut is poaching, clean the scallops by removing the tough membrane attached to the side of the muscle. Poach them in the simmering water for 1 to 2 minutes, then remove them to a plate to cool. Continue to keep the water simmering.

7. Poach the shrimp for 5 minutes. Remove to a plate to cool.

8. Remove any skin and bones from the poached fish. Flake the fish and place it, covered, in the refrigerator to chill. Cover the scallops and place them in the refrigerator to chill. Shell and devein the shrimp, cover them, and refrigerate. (The fish, scallops, and shrimp may all be placed on the same plate, but they should not be mixed together.)

9. Quarter and seed the melon and papaya. Peel and slice each quarter into 4 thin slices. Peel, trim, quarter, and core the pineapple. Cut each quarter crosswise into 4 slices. Place all the fruit together on a plate. Cover and set it aside.

10. Cook the noodles according to package directions. Drain the noodles, place them in a large bowl, and toss them with a quarter of the burgundy vinaigrette. Set aside. (All the separate parts of the salad can be made ahead up to this point. They should be kept separate and assembled just before serving.)

11. To serve: Toss the lettuce with ½ of the remaining Burgundy Vinaigrette. Place a bed of the dressed lettuce on a large plate or platter. Arrange a border of melon, papaya, and pineapple around the greens. Mound the cooked noodles in the center of the plate. Scatter the fish and scallops over the noodles. Arrange the shrimp around the edge of the noodles and pour the remaining vinaigrette over all. Serve immediately.

Avgolemono Timbales

YIELD: 6 SERVINGS AS AN ACCOMPANIMENT,
4 SERVINGS AS A LUNCHEON DISH

*T*hese special delectations are a molded version of the classic Greek egg-lemon soup. They're made from a light rice pilaf and a lemony custard, yielding a texture that's creamy and a taste that's fresh and light. They are a fine accompaniment to a festive, cooling dinner or a winning choice for a summer luncheon.

1 tablespoon butter for molds
1 medium onion
2 tablespoons olive oil
½ cup white rice
1 cup chicken stock
3 eggs
1 egg yolk
¾ cup light cream
½ teaspoon salt
¼ cup lemon juice
Freshly ground pepper to taste
Sprigs of fresh dill to garnish

1. Preheat the oven to 300° F.

2. Using the 1 tablespoon of butter, butter four ½-cup molds or 6 smaller molds, depending on whether you're serving this as a side dish or an entree.

3. Dice the onion. Place the oil in a medium saucepan over medium heat. Saute the onion, stirring occasionally, for 3 to 5 minutes, or until translucent. Add the rice to the saucepan and toss gently to coat it with oil. Continue cooking just until the rice is hot to the touch.

4. Pour the chicken stock over the rice and bring it to a boil. Lower the heat, cover the saucepan, and simmer the rice for 20 minutes, until all liquid is absorbed. Remove the saucepan from the heat, uncover it, and let the rice cool.

5. Place the eggs and extra egg yolk in a medium bowl and beat them for 1 to 2 minutes, until they are foamy. Mix in the cream and salt. Stirring, add the cooled rice, lemon juice, and pepper. Mix well.

6. Spoon the mixture into the buttered molds. Place the molds in a large baking dish and fill the dish with enough boiling water to come three quarters of the way up the sides of the molds. Cover the dish with foil and place it in the oven to bake for 20 to 25 minutes, until the timbales are set. Remove from the oven and let cool for 5 minutes. Unmold and garnish with the dill. Serve immediately, or cover and chill until serving time.

Key West Sponge Cake

YIELD: 1 8¼ × 4½-INCH LOAF OR 9-INCH CAKE

*I*t wasn't so long ago that it was difficult to lay hands on real Key lime juice, but then a Miami, Florida, firm called the Key West Lime Juice Factory became an important supplier of the nectar. Key lime pie's popularity soared. It just might be time for a Key lime alternative—and this same company has supplied us with a great dessert recipe. It's a light and tart sponge cake that can be topped beautifully with whipped cream and fresh berries of almost any kind. Or try it with Godiva Hot Fudge Sauce (see Index). It also makes an indulgent breakfast item, when sliced, toasted, and served with lime marmalade or a rich lemon curd.

Oil for pan
2 eggs
¾ cup sugar
⅛ teaspoon salt
5 tablespoons Key West (or other Key lime) Lime Juice
1 cup all-purpose flour
1½ teaspoons baking powder

1. Preheat the oven to 350° F.

2. Lightly oil an 8¼ × 4½-inch loaf pan or 9-inch cake pan. Set aside.

3. Separate the eggs. Place the egg whites in a small bowl and the egg yolks in the bowl of an electric mixer. Set aside the whites. Add the sugar and salt to the egg yolks and beat until fluffy. Continue to beat, adding the lime juice, 1 tablespoon at a time. Continue beating until the batter is thick and falls slowly off the beaters in a ribbon.

4. Beat the egg whites until firm. Add the beaten whites to the egg yolk mixture, along with the flour and baking powder. Fold gently with a spatula until combined.

5. Pour the batter into the prepared pan and bake 25 to 35 minutes, or until a skewer inserted in the center of the cake comes out dry. Invert the cake onto a rack and cool for at least five minutes.

Mount of Olives Spread

YIELD: ABOUT 1 CUP

*F*or centuries, workers in the olive groves of Greece have made a thick, nourishing spread to grace their noonday bread. Our version is excellent for hors d'oeuvres, on French bread or pita, even on crackers and cucumber rounds. This smooth-textured spread features the Mediterranean flavor of tapenade (black olive paste) and is easy to make ahead and to pack and take to a party.

1 medium tomato
1 small can tuna packed in olive oil (available in Italian markets and imported sections of supermarkets), drained
¼ cup tapenade or olivada (available in Italian markets or imported sections of supermarkets)
4 tablespoons butter
1 tablespoon lemon juice
Freshly ground pepper to taste
1 loaf crusty French bread
1 tablespoon chopped fresh Italian parsley

1. Core, seed, and dice the tomato. Set it aside.

2. Combine the tuna, tapenade, butter, lemon juice, and pepper in the bowl of a food processor fitted with a steel blade. Process until smooth. Pack the mixture in a crock, cover it, and refrigerate for at least 30 minutes.

3. When ready to serve, cut the French bread into ½-inch slices. Spread the tuna-olive mixture onto the bread. Top with a sprinkling of diced tomato and garnish with parsley. Serve immediately.

CLASSIC
MEDITERRANEAN MENU

Ouzo

Mount of Olives Spread

Moroccan Stuffed Leg of
Lamb

Herbed Vegetables Provençale

warmed pita triangles

Fluffy Avocado Cream

Greek Coffee

Moroccan Stuffed Leg of Lamb

YIELD: 6 TO 8 SERVINGS

Y ou'll definitely want to save this recipe for a special occasion. It makes a spectacular springtime dinner, but stuffing the lamb requires a little extra effort. The stuffing is so good you'll be glad to have the extra the recipe yields, which can be placed in a buttered baking dish, covered with foil, and heated in the oven with the lamb.

⅓ cup pine nuts (approximately 1 [2-ounce] jar)
1 cup couscous
2 tablespoons olive oil
1½ cups chicken stock or water
1 cup tiny peas, fresh or frozen and thawed
½ cup chopped fresh mint
½ teaspoon salt
Freshly ground pepper to taste
1 large (5- to 6-pound) leg of lamb, boned and untied
Butter for casserole (for extra stuffing)

1. Preheat the oven to 350° F.

2. Spread the pine nuts on a small ungreased baking sheet and toast in the oven for 5 to 7 minutes, or until golden. Remove the nuts from the oven and set them aside to cool.

3. Raise the oven temperature to 375° F.

4. Place the uncooked couscous in a medium bowl. Add 1 tablespoon of the oil and toss to coat.

5. Pour the chicken stock or water into a small saucepan. Place over medium-high heat and bring to a boil. Pour the hot stock or water over the couscous and stir. Cover and let stand for 5 minutes.

6. Add the peas, mint, salt, pepper, toasted pine nuts, and remaining oil to the couscous. Stir to combine.

7. Place the lamb on a large cutting board, with the fat side down. Place a layer of stuffing in the center of the lamb leg. Gather the meat around the stuffing and tie the leg with kitchen string. (This is much easier with two people—one to hold the meat together and one to tie the string.)

Fill a glass bowl with hand-painted Easter eggs, or place one in a glass egg holder or small votive cup at each place setting.

8. Place any extra stuffing in a buttered casserole dish and cover it with foil.

9. Place the tied lamb leg on a rack in a large roasting pan, with the fat side up. Roast for 1 to 1½ hours, or until a meat thermometer inserted into the center of the lamb reads 145° F. (The lamb will be quite pink, still.) Place the casserole dish of extra stuffing in the oven with the lamb for the last 30 to 40 minutes of cooking time. Remove the lamb from the oven and let it stand for 10 minutes, then slice and serve with the extra stuffing.

Herbed Vegetables Provençale

YIELD: 6 TO 8 SERVINGS

*I*n summer, serve these as a side dish at room temperature. In winter, serve them on an antipasto platter with cheeses, meats, olives, sun-dried tomatoes, and Italian bread.

2 large cloves garlic
½ cup red wine vinegar
1 cup olive oil
Salt and ground white pepper to taste
2 teaspoons dried rosemary (or 1 tablespoon chopped fresh)
6 small Italian eggplants
3 medium zucchini
3 medium summer squash
3 large red bell peppers
3 large green bell peppers
¼ cup chopped Italian parsley

1. Preheat the oven to 425° F.

2. Mince the garlic and place it in a large bowl. Add the wine vinegar and stir, then slowly whisk in the olive oil. Add the salt, white pepper, and rosemary and whisk well. Set dressing aside.

3. Trim the eggplants and cut them lengthwise into halves. Score each cut side lightly with the tip of a knife.

4. Quarter lengthwise the zucchini and summer squash. If desired, remove the seeds with the tip of a knife.

5. Cut the red and green peppers into quarters.

6. Whisk the dressing to reblend. Using tongs, dip the eggplant pieces into the dressing one piece at a time, and place the coated eggplant on a jelly roll pan or roasting pan. Repeat with the other vegetables, using one pan for the eggplant, a second for the zucchini and summer squash, and a third for the red and green peppers.

7. Roast the zucchini and summer squash and the peppers first. They should cook for 30 to 35 minutes. If your oven is large enough to hold the eggplant as well, add it to the oven after the squash and peppers have been roasting for 10 to 15 minutes. The eggplant should cook for 20 minutes. Using tongs, turn all the vegetables halfway through cooking, after 15 to 20 minutes, for the squash and peppers, and after 10 minutes for the eggplant.

8. When the vegetables are tender, remove them from the oven and arrange them on a large serving platter. Pour the juices from each pan over its respective vegetables, and sprinkle all with the chopped parsley. Serve immediately or store in the refrigerator, but return to room temperature before serving.

Fluffy Avocado Cream

YIELD: 4 TO 6 SERVINGS

*T*his surprising dessert takes only fifteen minutes from food processor to freezer. Served in wineglasses or layered with fresh strawberries parfait-style, it is a cool ending to a spring or summer meal.

Strawberry Compote (optional; recipe follows)
½ cup heavy cream, chilled
2 very ripe medium avocados
1 tablespoon lime juice
¼ cup confectioners' sugar
2 tablespoons kirsch (cherry brandy)
1 cup vanilla ice cream, softened

1. Make the Strawberry Compote, if desired.

2. Pour the chilled cream into a medium bowl and whip it just until soft peaks begin to form. Refrigerate.

3. Cut the avocados in half and remove the pits. Scoop the flesh into the bowl of a food processor fitted with a steel blade. Purée. Add the lime juice, sugar, and kirsch and pulse until well blended. Pour the mixture into a large bowl.

4. Place the softened ice cream in a separate small bowl and stir it just until it is of uniform texture. Using a spoon, fold the ice cream into the avocado mixture gently, keeping the bowl as cold as possible. (In a very hot kitchen, you may want to set the bowl in a pan of ice or ice water.)

5. Remove whipped cream from refrigerator and reblend. Lightly fold it into the avocado-ice cream mixture. Spoon it into dessert cups or glasses (use your sturdier goblets, so they'll withstand the cold) and place them in the freezer for at least 45 minutes and up to a day before serving. If you wish, you may layer the strawberry compote with the avocado cream like a parfait and freeze them together.

Strawberry Compote

1 pint fresh strawberries
2 tablespoons lime juice
½ cup sugar

1. Wash, hull, and slice the berries. Place them in a medium bowl.

2. Add the lime juice and sugar and toss to blend.

3. Allow the berry mixture to marinate for 15 to 30 minutes.

*T*here are as many kinds of parties as there are, well, party types—big and boisterous, or discreet and conversational. We can think of a million reasons for throwing a party, or attending one—a holiday office bash, an open house celebration, a bon voyage party, an engagement fete, a wedding reception, a christening, a bar mitzvah, a surprise birthday gathering, a neighborhood potluck supper. As long as there is life, there will always be a good excuse for a party.

Sometimes you're doing the giving and sometimes you're doing the going, but have been asked to bring more to the festivities than your engaging personality. Either way, you'll turn to these festive but simple recipes again and again—to beguile assembled friends and far-flung family members at your holiday buffet, and then enchant the guests at your law partner's surprise fortieth birthday party. Whether the occasion comes once a year or once a lifetime, these suggestions will make it more fun for everyone.

Crab and Green Onion Dip

YIELD: ABOUT 3 CUPS

Silly as it may sound, good dips are one of those things you never think about—until you need one. Well, here's a dip recipe that's a great improvement on a traditional hot crab dip. It's light and savory and should be served with sliced French bread or table water crackers.

1 medium bunch fresh parsley
1 medium bunch scallions
2 cloves garlic
1 cup mayonnaise
1 pound lump crabmeat
Salt to taste
¼ teaspoon ground white pepper
½ teaspoon Worcestershire sauce
2 tablespoons Key lime juice (at specialty food stores and in gourmet sections of many supermarkets)
2 tablespoons chopped fresh basil (or 2 teaspoons dried)
¼ cup grated Parmesan cheese

1. Preheat the broiler.

2. Remove the parsley stems, then chop the leaves coarsely and set aside.

3. Cut the scallions on the bias into ½-inch slices.

4. Chop the garlic coarsely.

5. Combine the parsley, scallions, and garlic in the bowl of a food processor fitted with a steel blade. Process to a medium chop.

6. Add the mayonnaise and process to blend.

7. Add the crabmeat, salt and pepper, Worcestershire sauce, lime juice, and basil. Process just to combine. (The dip may be made several hours ahead and refrigerated at this point. If you do so, preheat the broiler before you continue.)

8. Pile the dip into an ovenproof baking dish or pie plate. Sprinkle the Parmesan evenly over the entire surface. Broil, watching carefully, just until the top is golden brown.

9. Serve hot or lukewarm with sliced, toasted or untoasted French bread, or with table water crackers.

MAKING A GOOD CHEESE TRAY

Make an interesting cheese tray by mixing several different types, tastes, textures, and shapes, such as:

BONCHAMPS WITH MUSHROOMS

A rich and creamy cheese with the earthy flavor of mushrooms

PLAIN HAVARTI

A creamy, mild cheese with a buttery texture

SMOKED GOUDA

A firm cheese with a smoky flavor

COLBY

A semifirm domestic cheese, not too sharp

BOURSINE

A smooth-textured triple-crème cheese seasoned with herbs and garlic or pepper

Walnut-Eggplant Caviar

YIELD: ABOUT 4 CUPS

*T*his earthy dip, made from toasted walnuts and roasted eggplant, is a sophisticated accompaniment for crudités. It's also wonderful with toasted pita bread triangles.

½ pound shelled walnuts
1 (2½-pound) eggplant
2 medium onions
¼ cup walnut oil
3 cloves garlic
1 medium bunch fresh parsley
6 tablespoons lemon juice
Salt and freshly ground pepper to taste
½ teaspoon dried thyme

1. Preheat oven to 350°F.

2. Spread the walnuts in a single layer or an ungreased baking sheet. Toast in the oven for 10 minutes until well browned, tossing once. Remove from the oven and set aside.

3. Raise the oven temperature to 375° F.

4. Place the whole eggplant on a baking sheet and bake until soft when pierced with a knife, 45 to 60 minutes. Remove and cool.

5. While the eggplant is roasting, dice the onions. Sauté the onions in 1 tablespoon of the walnut oil in a small skillet over medium-high heat, for 3 to 4 minutes, until soft and translucent. Remove from the heat and cool.

6. Chop the garlic coarsely. Wash the parsley thoroughly and pat it dry. Remove and discard the stems, and chop the leaves coarsely.

7. Place the garlic, parsley, and onion in the bowl of a food processor fitted with a steel blade. Purée the mixture. Add the toasted walnuts and purée again. Add the remaining walnut oil, lemon juice, salt, thyme, and pepper, and pulse to combine.

8. Peel the cooled eggplant. Add the pulp to the walnut mixture in the food processor and purée until smooth. Serve as a dip with pita bread or crudités.

Aegean Cheese Wafers

YIELD: ABOUT 4 DOZEN

*I*n our snapping good cheese wafers, we substitute feta cheese and black olives for the traditional Cheddar and cayenne. Why not experiment yourself and try making them with blue cheese and toasted walnuts, or Gorgonzola and minced smoked ham?

½ cup packed oil-cured olives
¾ pound feta cheese
½ pound (1 cup) butter, room temperature
1½ cups flour
Freshly ground pepper to taste

1. Pit and chop the olives.

2. Crumble the feta cheese.

3. Place the butter in a medium bowl and beat it until it is creamy. Mix in the feta and olives. Add the flour and pepper, and blend well, kneading with your hands if necessary. Divide the dough in half and shape each half into a log. Wrap each log separately in plastic wrap, and refrigerate them for at least 1 hour.

4. When ready to bake, preheat the oven to 350° F.

5. Cut the logs into thin slices (⅛ inch) and place the slices on a non-stick baking sheet. Bake for 10 to 15 minutes, until they are browned and crisp. Remove from the oven and cool, or serve hot. Store in tins for 1 week or freeze. (You can also freeze the log uncooked, and cut off slices as you need them.)

THE PARTY PANTRY

Some wonderful items to have in your freezer, or on your pantry shelves, for last-minute hosting:

♦ Smoked clams or oysters—in a pinch, you can serve them with nothing but toothpicks, but they are especially good with water crackers or some other plain cracker, and they are delicious tossed with pasta or sprinkled in salads.

♦ Canned pâté or Brie—both are available in specialty stores and import sections of many supermarkets and both are actually good!

♦ Spiced cashews, almonds, or pecans—perennial favorites that are great for munching with cocktails. Make them yourself or buy them already spiced.

♦ A frozen log of Aegean Cheese Wafers can be sliced easily while still frozen, and the wafers baked without waiting for them to thaw.

♦ Canned escargots with frozen Herb-Garlic Butter (see Index for Compound Butters), and a refrigerator loaf of soft breadsticks (the kind that pop out of the can when you twist it). Just layer the escargots in a shallow baking dish (or escargot pan, if you have one), dot each with some herb butter, and put them in the oven with the breadsticks. Serve them together for an appetizer that seems anything but spontaneous.

Terry's Pirated Bermuda Fish Stew

YIELD: 12 TO 14 SERVINGS

*T*he story of how this most unusual fish stew found its way from the jewel of the Atlantic to the North Shore of Boston is a rather colorful yarn which involved a chef from St. George and several applications of Black Seal Rum and Coke. Well, mate, it's a tale we don't have time to spin. Suffice to say, a pleasantly devious science teacher with a great palate and a good memory for details brought this recipe home with him from a Bermuda sojourn and we're all the luckier for his larceny. The recipe is a bit time-consuming, but can be made well in advance or in stages. It's really a meal in itself, great for caroling parties or a Saturday night at home with a gang of friends.

STOCK:
3 small sole frames (racks) or 1 large haddock or cod frame
  (sole is best, as it has more flavor and is less bony)
    see note)
2 teaspoons salt
2 bay leaves
2 teaspoons ground allspice
1 teaspoon dried thyme
1 teaspoon black peppercorns
1 teaspoon ground cloves
1 stick cinnamon

NOTE: The frame (rack) consists of the head, bones, and trimmings.

SOUP:
6 slices bacon
2 large yellow onions
2 medium bell peppers, any color
6 medium stalks celery
2 large cloves garlic
4 medium potatoes (Russett are good because they are firm)
1 small yellow turnip
6 medium carrots
1½ teaspoons curry powder
1 large can (1 pound, 12 ounces) peeled, whole tomatoes
2 cups chicken stock
1 cup ketchup

1 small bottle (approximately 9 ounces) mango chutney
2 tablespoons Worcestershire sauce
2 tablespoons lemon juice
Several dashes sherry hot pepper sauce, such as Outer Bridges
    Sherry Hot Pepper Sauce
½ cup dark rum (preferably Myers's or Black Seal)
¼ cup dry sherry

FISH:
3 pounds cusk, ocean perch, or other firm-textured white
    fish
½ cup chopped fresh Italian parsley
Dark rum to taste (see suggestion above)
Sherry hot pepper sauce to taste (see suggestion above)

1. To make the stock, have the fishmonger gut the frames, if necessary. Rinse the frames well and place them in a large, non-aluminum stockpot.

2. Fill the pot with enough water to cover the racks. Add the salt, bay leaves, ground allspice, thyme, peppercorns, cloves, and cinnamon.

3. Bring the liquid to a boil over high heat. Lower the heat and simmer, covered, for 30 minutes.

4. Strain the stock into a large bowl or other large pot. Discard the racks, bay leaves, and anything else that doesn't go through the strainer. Rinse the stockpot, then return the stock to the pot. (If you wish, the stock may be prepared ahead up to this point. Let the stock cool to lukewarm, then refrigerate it overnight.)

5. Place the bacon slices in a large heavy stockpot over low heat. Slowly render the bacon slices until crisp.

6. If you have prepared the stock ahead and refrigerated it, place it over low heat to warm.

7. While the bacon cooks, dice the onions, peppers, and celery. Mince the garlic.

8. Remove the bacon and reserve it for another use. Add the onions, peppers, celery, and garlic to the bacon fat and sauté, stirring occasionally, until the onions are translucent and the vegetables are soft, for about 5 minutes.

9. While the onion mixture is cooking, cut the potatoes and turnip into ½-inch cubes. Cut the carrots into ⅓-inch cubes.

10. Add the curry powder to the onion mixture and sauté for 1 minute without browning. Pour the warm stock over the onion mixture and stir to combine, scraping the pan well to deglaze. Add the potatoes, turnip, and carrots. Chop the tomatoes or squeeze them through your hands over the soup to break them into chunks. Add them to the soup, along with any liquid from the can. Add the chicken stock, ketchup, chutney, Worcestershire sauce, lemon juice, and sherry hot pepper sauce. Stir to combine. Bring the liquid to a boil, then lower the heat and simmer, covered, for 2 hours.

11. Add the rum and sherry and cook for another 30 minutes. (If you wish, you may make the stew ahead to this point also. Let it cool to room temperature, then refrigerate for 1 to 2 days.)

12. About 30 minutes before serving, place the stew over low heat and warm gently, then raise the heat to medium-high and bring the liquid to a boil.

13. Cut the fish into 1- to 2-inch chunks. Add the fish to the pot and return the stew to a boil, then lower the heat and simmer, covered, for 10 to 15 minutes, until the fish is cooked. Stir in the chopped parsley. Ladle the stew into serving bowls. Pass rum and sherry hot pepper sauce for each person to pour on freely.

Mini Date Muffins with Smoked Ham

YIELD: 36 MINI MUFFINS

*P*eople just can't seem to get enough of fresh baked muffins. Here's a versatile recipe that looks great piled up on a pretty tray at a buffet or brunch, and is terrific for picnics and working lunches, too.

¾ cup pineapple juice
½ cup water
1 (8-ounce) package chopped dates
1 tablespoon oil for muffin tin
3 tablespoons butter
1 cup sugar

1 large egg
3 cups flour
1 teaspoon baking soda
1 teaspoon baking powder
¼ teaspoon salt
Honey mustard
8 to 10 thin slices of smoked ham

1. Preheat the oven to 375° F.

2. Combine the pineapple juice and water in a small saucepan. Bring the liquid to a boil. Place the chopped dates in a medium bowl and pour the hot liquid over them. Stir the mixture and let it stand until lukewarm.

3. Brush a miniature muffin tin with the oil. Set it aside.

4. Melt the butter in a small saucepan over moderate heat. Place the sugar in a medium bowl. Add the melted butter and mix to combine. Add the egg and beat.

5. Sift the flour, baking soda, and baking powder over the sugar mixture. Add the salt and dates to the mixture, and stir everything together just to combine.

6. Fill the muffin tins to the top with batter. Bake the muffins for 15 to 20 minutes, or until a skewer inserted in the center of the muffins comes out clean and dry. Remove them from the oven, turn them out of the tins, and let the muffins cool on a rack. Repeat, brushing the tin and filling it, and baking, until you have used all the batter.

7. When the muffins are cool, slice them in half across and spread each side with the honey mustard. Pile a slice of smoked ham on each bottom half and top with the top half. Serve at once, or cover and refrigerate until serving time, but return the muffins to room temperature first.

Mild Wild Rice with Smoked Turkey and Tangerines

YIELD: 8 TO 12 SERVINGS

Good party recipes are a challenge to find—and sometimes to make. This one is easy to put together and has the double benefit of being not only a great addition to a potluck supper or an elegant buffet, but also a salad your family can munch on for days straight from the refrigerator. Packs superbly in a lunch box, too.

DRESSING:
¾ cup red wine vinegar
1½ tablespoons Dijon-style mustard
Salt and freshly ground pepper
¾ cup olive oil
½ cup vegetable oil

SALAD:
½ cup wild rice
2 cups white rice
2 pounds smoked turkey
8 tangerines
1 cup chopped fresh Italian parsley (about 1 small bunch)
Boston or red leaf lettuce leaves for garnish

1. To make the dressing, mix the vinegar, mustard, salt and pepper together in a small bowl. Slowly whisk the olive oil and vegetable oil into the vinegar mixture. Set aside.

2. To make the salad, cook the 2 rices separately, according to their package directions. When cooked, combine the rices in a large bowl and set aside to cool.

3. Cut the smoked turkey into ⅓-inch julienne.

4. Peel and section 6 tangerines (reserve 2 tangerines for garnish). Cut a small slit in the seed side of the section (the flat side), and remove the seeds by squeezing gently.

5. Add the turkey, tangerine sections, and parsley to the rice. Pour the dressing over the rice mixture and toss well.

6. For the garnishes, peel and slice the remaining two tangerines into 6 slices each. Remove the seeds as before. Wash and dry the lettuce leaves.

7. To assemble, place the lettuce leaves on individual salad plates. Place a scoop of salad on each lettuce leaf and garnish with a tangerine slice.

Chili Tartlettes with Cheese

YIELD: 3 DOZEN TARTLETTES

We've added cornmeal to the tart shell of this fantastic hors d'oeuvres or party food, to give it an extra bit of crunch and more Southwestern flavor. You can allow the heat of the chili to melt the cheese slightly or else broil the tarts after you add the cheese, a good thing to do if you want to make them ahead and reheat just before serving. Following are recipes for two other tartlette fillings—red onion and sausage.

TARTLETTE PASTRY:
1½ cups flour, sifted
½ cup cornmeal or corn flour
1 teaspoon salt
¾ cup chilled butter
⅓ cup ice water (approximately)

FILLING:
3 cups Bildner's Chili (see Index; about ¼ of the recipe)
1 cup grated Monterey Jack cheese

1. To make the pastry, mix together in a large bowl the flour, cornmeal or corn flour, and salt.

2. Using a pastry blender or two knives, cut the butter into the flour mixture, until the mixture has the texture of a coarse (pea-sized) meal.

3. Sprinkle the water over the meal, 1 tablespoon at a time, and toss with a fork. When the dough starts to come together (this may occur before you have used all the water, or you may have to add 1 or 2 tablespoons, depending on the brand of flour used), gently press together to form a ball, flatten slightly, and wrap in plastic. Refrigerate the dough for at least 30 minutes.

4. When the dough is thoroughly chilled, place it on a floured board and roll it out to a thickness of ⅛-inch. Using a tart or biscuit cutter, cut the dough into 3¼-inch circles. Place the circles in a jam tart plaque or plaques. Place any extra circles on a lightly floured cookie sheet. Place the jam tart plaque and extra circles in the refrigerator to chill for 30 minutes.

5. Preheat the oven to 375° F.

6. Bake the tartlettes for 10 minutes, keeping the extra circles chilled. When the tartlettes are very lightly browned, remove them from the oven and let them cool in the pan for 2 to 3 minutes. Gently remove them from the pan and place them on a rack or plate. Refill the plaque with the chilled extra circles, and repeat until all the tartlettes are baked.

7. To make the filling, heat the chili in a medium saucepan over low heat.

8. When bubbling, place a tablespoon of chili in each tartlette. Top each with approximately 1 teaspoon of grated cheese. Serve immediately, or place the tartlettes on a cookie sheet, then broil in the oven for 2 minutes just before serving, to reheat them and melt the cheese.

Red Filling for Tartlettes

YIELD: 3 DOZEN TARTLETTES

1 recipe Tartlette Pastry (see Chili Tartlettes with Cheese)
4 medium to large red onions
4 tablespoons butter
Salt to taste
1 cup red wine
Freshly ground pepper to taste

1. Cut the onion into ⅛-inch slices.

2. Melt the butter in a large skillet over medium heat. Add the sliced onions and salt and toss to coat. Cook, stirring occasionally, for 3 to 5 minutes, until the onions are translucent.

3. Add the wine, bring the liquid to a boil, then reduce the heat to low. Simmer the onions until the wine is nearly completely absorbed. Season with black pepper to taste. Spoon into tartlette shells and serve.

Sausage Filling for Tartlettes

YIELD: 3 DOZEN TARTLETTES

1 recipe Tartlette Pastry (see Chili Tartlettes with Cheese)
1 medium onion
1 tablespoon olive oil
2 pounds sweet sausage
Salt and freshly ground pepper to taste
¼ cup red wine vinegar
¼ cup raisins or currants
¼ cup water
4 tablespoons tomato paste

1. Dice the onion.

2. Heat the oil in a large skillet over medium-high heat. Sauté the onion, stirring often, for 3 minutes, until translucent.

3. Add the sausage and cook, stirring to break up any chunks. Season with salt and pepper.

4. When the sausage is browned, pour the fat from the skillet and add the vinegar, raisins or currants, water, and tomato paste. Stir to combine.

5. Bring the mixture to a boil. Continue to cook for a few minutes, until the sauce is reduced enough to coat the sausage. Spoon into the tartlette shells and serve.

Festive Holiday Bird

YIELD: 6 SQUABS, 2 PHEASANTS,
1 LARGE ROASTING CHICKEN, OR 1 TURKEY

A well-cooked bird can often mean the difference between a gracious holiday buffet and just another Christmas party. Here's a versatile recipe that can be used for chicken, turkey, goose, pheasant, squab, even game hens. Stuffed with a bread stuffing flavored with roasted pine nuts, a hint of orange, and chocolate, your bird will be succulent and memorable.

½ cup pine nuts
2 medium onions
2 medium stalks celery
½ cup butter plus 1 tablespoon for baking dish
1½ ounces unsweetened chocolate
2 medium oranges
1 (1-pound) loaf firm-textured bread (white or half whole wheat, half white)
½ cup chicken stock
½ cup heavy cream
1 teaspoon dried tarragon
1 teaspoon dried oregano
1 teaspoon dried thyme
1 teaspoon dried marjoram
½ teaspoon ground cinnamon
½ teaspoon ground coriander
¼ teaspoon ground cloves
1 teaspoon salt
Freshly ground pepper to taste
¼ cup sherry
1 (5- to 6-pound) roasting chicken or 2 pheasants or 6 (1-pound) squabs or a small turkey
½ cup orange juice
2 tablespoons thawed frozen orange juice concentrate

1. Preheat the oven to 350° F.

2. Place the pine nuts on an ungreased cookie sheet or cake pan and toast for 5 to 10 minutes, until golden. Remove from the oven and let cool.

3. Keep the oven at 350° F.

4. Cut the onion and celery into ¼-inch dice. Melt ½ cup of the butter in a sauté pan over medium-high heat. Add the onion and celery and cook until soft, 2 to 3 minutes.

5. Place the chocolate in a small heatproof bowl over simmering water, and melt it while the onion cooks.

6. Grate the orange rind and place it in a large bowl.

7. Break the bread into pea-sized pieces and add it to the orange rind. Add the stock and heavy cream and mix to moisten the bread.

8. Add the herbs and spices, salt, pepper, and sherry to the bread mixture. Add the reserved nuts, sautéed vegetables, and melted chocolate and mix everything together thoroughly.

9. Butter a large casserole dish with the remaining 1 tablespoon butter. Pile the stuffing into the buttered dish and set aside.

10. Place the bird or birds on a rack in a roasting pan.

11. In a small bowl, mix the orange juice with the orange juice concentrate.

12. Brush the bird or birds with the orange juice mixture and roast, basting every 15 minutes, according to the following timetable: chicken: 1½ hours; pheasant: 25 minutes per pound; squab: 45 minutes to 1 hour; turkey: 15 minutes per pound.

13. Place the stuffing in the oven to bake for the last 45 minutes of the bird's cooking time, or until golden brown on top and piping hot inside. The stuffing should be timed to come out of the oven with the chosen bird.

Creamy Orange Cauliflower

YIELD: 6 TO 8 SERVINGS

*T*his is an easy but elegant make-ahead vegetable that would be just perfect for a dinner party or a holiday buffet. The orange sauce is really a mayonnaise, so it should not be allowed to sit at room temperature for too long. Any extra orange dressing makes a delicious topping for cold chicken or ham sandwiches, or is a nice change in a simple chicken salad.

1 large head cauliflower
1 (3 × 1-inch) strip orange rind
¼ cup orange juice
2 tablespoons frozen orange juice concentrate, thawed
¼ teaspoon turmeric
Salt and freshly ground pepper to taste
2 egg yolks
½ cup olive oil
½ cup safflower oil
1 scallion, green part only

1. Break the cauliflower into flowerets. Steam or boil them just until tender, about 10 minutes. Place in a large serving bowl to cool.

2. While the cauliflower cooks and cools, place the orange rind, orange juice, thawed concentrate, turmeric, salt, and pepper in a blender. Blend until the rind is finely chopped. Add the egg yolks one at a time and blend until smooth after each. With the blender running on low, add the olive oil and the safflower oil very gradually. Continue to blend slowly until the mixture is homogeneous.

3. Toss the cauliflower with just enough dressing to coat (the amount will vary depending on the size of the cauliflower head you have used, so just continue to add small amounts of dressing and toss until all the cauliflower is coated). Cut the scallions on the bias into thin slices. Sprinkle the sliced scallions over the salad. Serve immediately or store in the refrigerator, then return to room temperature before serving.

Low Country Sweet Potatoes

YIELD: 8 SERVINGS

A Southerner who works for us speaks with fondness of Sunday luncheons at his family's home in rural North Carolina—and his particular passion for a zesty potato dish very much like this one. This recipe is a great change of pace for holiday entertaining, or simply a terrific way to dress up any autumn meal. It can be made ahead and refrigerated before baking.

2 teaspoons minced fresh ginger
1½ cups orange juice
1½ cups chicken stock
3 tablespoons lemon juice
3 large sweet potatoes
4 tablespoons butter
¾ cup coarsely chopped dates
Salt and ground white pepper to taste

1. Preheat the oven to 375° F.

2. Place the ginger in a medium bowl. Mix in the orange juice, chicken stock, and lemon juice.

3. Peel the sweet potatoes and cut them into ⅛-inch slices.

4. Grease the bottom and sides of a large baking or casserole dish with 1 teaspoon of the butter.

5. Spread one third of the sweet potatoe slices in a layer in the bottom of the buttered dish. Scatter one third of the dates over the potatoes. Dot with one-third of the remaining butter, and sprinkle with salt and white pepper.

6. Repeat the layers twice, using half of the remaining ingredients for each layer. Finish by sprinkling salt and white pepper over the top.

7. Pour the chicken stock mixture over all the layers. Bake, uncovered, for 1 hour to 1 hour, 15 minutes, until the potatoes are tender and the juices have the consistency of a sauce. Serve hot.

THE SWEETEST POTATO STORY IN HISTORY

They're really not sweet potatoes at all, but members of the morning glory family that, among other things, are packed with vitamin A. But to some extent at least, Americans have them to thank for helping their ancestors survive the difficult years when this country was first settled. Sweet potatoes not only served as a primary staple food in the diet of early North American settlers, showing up in everything from breakfast mush to Christmas dinner (as they did in the diets of the earliest North Americans—namely, the Indians), but also served as feed and life-support staple for livestock. Sweet potatoes also played a big role in sustaining the diet of the war-torn South following the traumatic years of the Civil War.

Cranberry-Cabernet Relish

YIELD: 2½ TO 3 CUPS

*I*t's unfortunate that even the most creative cooks think of cranberries only at Thanksgiving, as they are superior for dressing up meats and poultry dishes year round. That said, this easy relish unquestionably makes a lovely addition to the holiday dinner table.

1 medium seedless orange
1 teaspoon minced fresh ginger
12 ounces fresh cranberries (approximately 1 bag)
½ cup light brown sugar, lightly packed
1 tablespoon molasses
1 cup cabernet sauvignon
¼ cup golden raisins
¼ cup raisins
½ stick cinnamon
4 whole cloves
6 whole allspice berries (or ½ teaspoon ground)

1. Peel the orange. Divide it into sections and cut each section into 8 pieces.

2. Combine the orange, ginger, cranberries, and brown sugar in a heavy saucepan. Add the molasses and the cabernet sauvignon and stir. Mix in both kinds of raisins.

3. Place the cinnamon stick, cloves, and allspice in a sachet bag or cheesecloth bag and add it to the mixture.

4. Bring to a boil over high heat. Lower the heat to a simmer and cook, uncovered, until the cranberries are tender, about 10 minutes. Cool to room temperature and remove the sachet or cheesecloth bag before serving.

Gingered Pear Chutney

YIELD: ABOUT 2 CUPS

*T*he making of chutneys is, we think, something of a lost art form. This robust chutney is fabulous on grilled chicken or roast pork, to top off a country-style pâté, or simply by itself on the buffet table. You can make it well in advance of a party, and it makes an appreciated gift.

½ pound apples (approximately 1 large)
2 pounds pears (approximately 4 medium)
1 large onion
1 ounce fresh ginger
½ cup lightly packed light brown sugar
½ cup sugar
2 tablespoons molasses
1 cup vinegar (preferably pear, if available)
1 stick cinnamon
2 whole cloves
6 allspice berries (or ½ teaspoon ground)
¼ cup currants
¼ cup golden raisins
½ teaspoon salt
1 cup water

1. Peel, core, and dice the apple and pears.

2. Dice the onion.

3. Mince the ginger.

4. Combine the apple, pear, onion, and ginger in a large heavy saucepan with all the remaining ingredients. Bring the mixture to a boil over high heat. Lower the heat and simmer, covered, the chutney for 1 to 2 hours, until the fruit is tender and the juices are syrupy.

5. Remove the saucepan from the heat and let the chutney cool to room temperature. Serve immediately or refrigerate until serving time. Will keep well up to 2 weeks, stored tightly covered and refrigerated.

Chocolate Panettone
Bread Pudding

YIELD: 1 (10-INCH) PIE PLATE OR ROUND CASSEROLE DISH

*T*his recipe is a holiday gem. Panettone can often be found in Italian markets and specialty shops year-round, and at regular supermarkets around the holiday season. Leftover panettone makes delicious French toast, and is delicious simply toasted and spread with Cranberry-Cabernet Relish (see Index).

2 tablespoons butter, softened
4 (1-ounce) wedges, panettone (about 1½ inches across at wide end)
1 ounce semisweet chocolate
2 tablespoons unsweetened cocoa powder
2 tablespoons confectioners' sugar
2½ cups evaporated milk
4 large eggs
¾ cup heavy cream, chilled
1 teaspoon ground cinnamon

1. Preheat the oven to 325° F.

2. Spread the softened butter over both sides of each panettone slice. Cut each slice in half diagonally. Arrange the slices in a concentric pattern in a 10-inch pie plate or round casserole dish. Set aside.

3. Place the chocolate in a medium heatproof bowl over a saucepan of water. Place the saucepan over medium heat until the water gets hot enough to melt the chocolate. Remove from the heat. Whisk the cocoa, confectioners' sugar, and milk into the melted chocolate. Place the saucepan back over low heat and stir until the mixture is warm. Remove from the heat.

4. In a medium bowl, whisk the eggs until fluffy. Continuing to whisk, slowly pour the chocolate mixture into the eggs. Whisk until smooth. Pour the mixture through a colander or strainer over the panettone slices.

5. Carefully place dish on the middle rack of the oven. Bake until the custard is almost set, 15 to 20 minutes. Remove from the oven and cool on a rack.

6. Pour the whipping cream into a medium bowl and whip until soft peaks begin to form. Add the cinnamon and whip until firm. Refrigerate.

7. Serve the pudding warm or chilled. Top with the cinnamon-flavored whipped cream.

Pacific Star Cake

YIELD: 1 (9-INCH) CAKE

*T*his upside-down cake should be served slightly warm and sticky. So plan to take it out of the oven just before the guests begin eating dinner, or reheat it in the microwave just before serving.

4 ounces dried apricots
½ cup butter, room temperature
¾ cup brown sugar
2 large star fruit (carambolas, found at specialty markets and many supermarkets)
¾ cup sugar
¼ teaspoon salt
3 large eggs
½ teaspoon vanilla
½ cup orange juice
1½ cups flour
1 teaspoon baking powder
Whipped cream for topping

1. Preheat the oven to 350° F.

2. Cover the dried apricots with boiling water and let them soak.

3. In a small saucepan, melt ¼ cup of the butter. When it is melted, stir in the brown sugar. Spread the mixture evenly over the bottom of a 9-inch round cake pan.

4. Cut the unpeeled star fruit crosswise into ¼-inch slices. Drain the apricots and place them on a paper towel to absorb any excess moisture. Arrange the apricots and star fruit in concentric pattern over the brown sugar mixture, alternating rows of star fruit with rows of apricots. Set aside.

5. In the bowl of an electric mixer, place the remaining ¼ cup of butter with the sugar and salt. Beat at medium speed to cream.

6. While the butter mixture is creaming, separate the eggs. Place the eggs whites in a large bowl and add the yolks to the butter-sugar mixture one at a time, beating well after each. Add the vanilla and beat.

7. Reduce speed to slow and add the orange juice. (The mixture will separate, but do not worry. It will recombine when the flour is added.) Turn the mixer off and add the flour and baking powder. Using a spoon, stir gently just to combine.

8. Beat the egg whites until stiff. Using a spatula, fold them into the batter.

9. Pour the batter into the pan over the fruit, sealing the batter to the edge of the pan. Bake for 30 to 35 minutes, until the top is golden and a skewer inserted in the cake comes out clean and dry.

10. Turn the cake out immediately onto a cake rack set over a serving platter. Let the cake cool to warm, then slide it onto the serving platter. Serve warm with whipped cream.

Appetizers and Hors d-Oeuvres

Aegean Cheese Wafers
Cajun Meatballs
Chicken Liver Apple Pâté with Cognac
Chili Tartlettes with Cheese
Chipped Chicken Wings
Crab and Green Onion Dip
Hot Chèvre Rounds with Basil and Sun-dried Tomatoes
Hot Grilled Littlenecks
Marinated Tortellini with Basil-Sour Cream Dip
Mason-Dixon Croutons
Mini Date Muffins with Smoked Ham
Morel Roulades
Mount of Olives Spread
Red Filling for Tartlettes
Sausage Filling for Tartlettes
Smoked Oyster Toasts with Herb Butter
Southwestern Cherry Tomatoes
Steve's Guacamole Salsa
Trombly's Peanut Butter Pâté
Walnut-Eggplant Caviar

Soups

Barley Soup with Shiitake Mushrooms and Dill
Bildner's Famous Clam Chowder
German Potato Soup with Bacon and Onion
Joan's Gazpacho
Spiced Fruit Soup
Terry's Pirated Bermuda Fish Stew

Salads

Bildner's Famous Red Potato Salad
Gold Rush Coleslaw
Health Salad
Italian Tuna Salad
Pasta Salad with Shrimp and Pine Nuts
Red Rufus Salad
Seafood Salad with Tropical Fruits
Smoked Salad with Prickly Pears
Southwest Salad Bowl
Summer Salmon Salad
Szechwan Lo Mein Salad with Spicy Peanut Sauce
Wild Blue Salad

Seafood

Bildner's Famous Clam Chowder
Casablanca Ragout with Sweet Corn and Bell Pepper
Chardonnay-Poached Salmon with Ginger and Three-Mustard Sauce
Crab and Green Onion Dip
Dry-Marinated Swordfish with Tomato-Lime Relish
Honey-Lemon Baked Salmon
Hot Grilled Littlenecks
Italian Tuna Salad
Mount of Olives Spread
Pasta Salad with Shrimp and Pine Nuts
Sautéed Scallops with Tequila and Lime
Seafood Salad with Tropical Fruits
South Pacific Shrimp
Steamed Lobster
Summer Salmon Salad
Terry's Pirated Bermuda Fish Stew

Poultry

Baja Chicken
Baked Chicken Breasts with Nectarine
Chicken Pot Pie
Chinatown Roast Duckling
Chipped Chicken Wings
Festive Holiday Bird
Lemon Chicken
Louisiana Tenderloins
Mango Chicken Breasts with Cardamom Sauce
Martini-Grilled Quail
Spicy Peanut Chicken

Meat

The Bildner Burger
Bildner's Chili
Brandied Tenderloin with Bacon and Peppercorns
Bourbon-Glazed Stuffed Pork Loin
Cajun Meatloaf
Casablanca Ragout with Sweet Corn and Bell Pepper
Country Ham and Crab with Cider
Flank Steak with Sesame-Cilantro Marinade
Hazelnut-Baked Pork Chops
Irish Lasagna
Moroccan Stuffed Leg of Lamb
New Age Steak and Cheese
Red Cabbage Harvest Rolls
Roast Tenderloin with Watercress Butter
Texas-Style BBQ Brisket of Beef
Veal Chops with Special Cognac Sauce
Veal Goulash with Garlic and Caraway
Veal Scallops with Garlic and Artichokes

Pasta, Rice, and Grains

Avgolemono Timbales
Baked Grits with Chives
Bowtie Noodles and Poppyseed Butter
Health Salad
Marinated Tortellini with Basil-Sour Cream Dip
Mild Wild Rice with Smoked Turkey and Tangerines
Orzo with Parsley and Garlic
Pasta Salad with Shrimp and Pine Nuts
Szechwan Lo Mein Salad with Spicy Peanut Sauce
Tidewater Rice
Tzatziki Couscous

Potatoes

Bildner's Famous Red Potato Salad
Cross-Country Baked Potatoes
   Midwestern Stuffed Potatoes
   New England Stuffed Potatoes
   Southern Stuffed Potatoes
   Southwestern Stuffed Potatoes
German Potato Soup with Bacon and Onion
Hot Potato Pepper Salad
Irish Lasagna
Low Country Sweet Potatoes
Sage-Roasted Potatoes
Sliced Potato and Onion Pie

Vegetables

Asparagus with Citrus Butter
Carolina Carrots
Christmas Enchiladas
Creamy Orange Cauliflower
Herbed Vegetables Provençale
Low Country Sweet Potatoes
Mixed Greens and Canadian Bacon
Roasted Eggplant with Garlic and Lemon
Southwestern Souffléed Tomatoes
Yellow Beans with Roasted Pecan Dressing

Desserts

Afternoon Apple Bars
Almond Genoise
American Bounty Cobbler
Banana-Mocha Cupcakes
Caramel Pudding Cake
Cherry-Meringue "Shortcake"
Chocolate Panettone Bread Pudding
Cocoa Cream
Coconut-Baked Pears
Coffee-Macadamia Freeze with Espresso-Chocolate Sauce
Cream Cheese Apple Pie
Emma's Grand Marnier Ice Cream
Fluffy Avocado Cream
Godiva Angel Pie
Godiva Hot Fudge Sauce
Key West Sponge Cake
Lisa's Lemon-Butter Bars
Meringue Stars
Mother's Warm Applesauce
Not Just Another Pretty Peanut Butter Pie
Pacific Star Cake
Perfect Peach Cheesecake
Pumpkin Ginger Cheesecake
The Richest Lunch Box Cookies Ever
Sorry, Bill, Chocolate Pudding
Strawberry Compote
Summer Sabayon
Two-Lime Mousse
Vanilla-Eggnog Custard Sauce
Wedding Cake Sorbet with Champagne

Brunches and Breakfasts

Baked Grits with Chives
Banana-Mocha Cupcakes
Bildner Benedict
Corn, Brie, and Jalapeño Frittata
Down-Home Waffles
Egg and Toasted Almonds on Black Bread
Golden Island Scones
High-Stress Shake
Hot Potato Pepper Salad
Italian Bacon and Eggs
Key West Sponge Cake
Lemon Pear Bread
McSteven's Cocoa Muffins
Make-Ahead Morning Muffins
Mini Date Muffins with Smoked Ham
Peachy-Cheese Jamboree Pancakes
Quick Bacon Bread
A Romantic Russian Omelet
Runner's Shake
Southwestern Souffléed Tomatoes
Sunday French Toast
Vanilla-Eggnog Custard Sauce
Yankee Griddle Corn Cakes

Lunch

American Sushi
   Cream Cheese with Nuts and Raisins
   Ham and Beans
   Roast Beef and Asparagus with Horseradish Dressing
Avgolemono Timbales
Cross-Country Baked Potatoes
   Midwestern Stuffed Potatoes
   New England Stuffed Potatoes
   Southern Stuffed Potatoes
   Southwestern Stuffed Potatoes
Fluffy Horseradish Dressing
Health Salad
Hot Potato Pepper Salad
Italian Tuna Salad
Joan's Gazpacho
Mini Date Muffins with Smoked Ham
New Age Steak and Cheese
Southwestern Souffléed Tomatoes

Breads, Muffins, and Scones

Banana-Mocha Cupcakes
Golden Island Scones
Lemon Pear Bread
McSteven's Cocoa Muffins
Make-Ahead Morning Muffins
Mini Date Muffins with Smoked Ham
Quick Bacon Bread
Spicy Corn Bread

Beverages

Harvard-Yale Hot Buttered Rum Mix
Rick and Susie's Day at the Beach

Sauces and Condiments

Basil-Sour Cream Dip
Burgundy Vinaigrette
Chocolate-Pecan Cream
Cranberry-Cabernet Relish
Espresso-Chocolate Sauce
Fluffy Horseradish Dressing
Gingered Pear Chutney
Godiva Hot Fudge Sauce
Hazelnut Pesto Sauce
Herb Butter
Mother's Warm Apple Sauce
Pear Cream
Raspberry Cream
Raspberry-Wine Dressing
Sesame-Cilantro Marinade
Spicy Peanut Sauce
Steve's Guacamole Salsa
Three-Mustard Sauce
Tomato-Lime Relish
Vanilla-Eggnog Custard Sauce
Whipped Bourbon Cream

INDEX

About the Authors

*I*n his early thirties, Jim Bildner set out to reinvent the neighborhood grocery store. Today, his eighteen stores in Boston, Chicago, and Atlanta are spoiling customers with premium groceries, high standards of service, stylish settings, and a wide range of take-out and catered foods.

His ideas about service and quality come from a family tradition; his grandfather, Joe Bildner, founded King's Super Markets in northern New Jersey.

The staff of food experts at J. Bildner & Sons have brought to this book their knowledge, creativity, and belief that food can make special every part of life.

James Dodson, senior writer for *Yankee Magazine*, has written about food and other interesting subjects for the last fifteen years.